A Busy Person's Guide to the

20 MINUTE GARDEN

A Busy Person's Guide to the

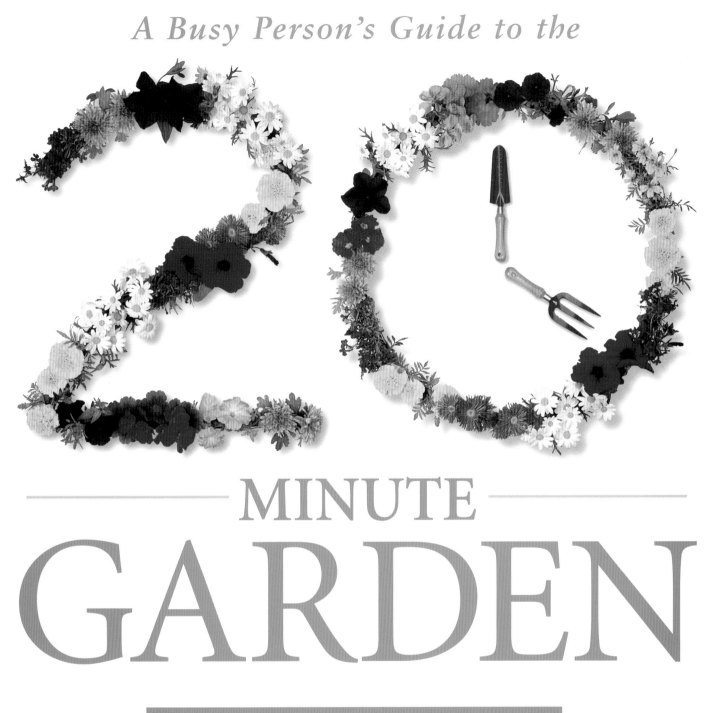

20
— MINUTE —
GARDEN

GILL PAGE

Abbeydale Press

Above: Alchemilla mollis *provides useful and attractive ground cover around the base of a container planted with an* Acer japonicum.

Published in 2000 by
ABBEYDALE PRESS
An imprint of Bookmart Limited
Desford Road
Enderby
Leicester LE9 5AD

ISBN 1-86147-029-0

Reprinted 2001, 2002

Edited and designed by Ideas Into Print
Kent DA3 8JD, England

Practical photography by Geoffrey Rogers

Colour reproduction by Sino Publishing House Ltd,
Hong Kong

Printed in Singapore

Contents

Above: *Create a spot in the garden where you can sit peacefully and take the time to decide what needs doing. Learning about your garden means making the right decisions, not time-wasting ones.*

Introduction

Busy people need time to unwind and there is no better place to do that than in the garden. Gardens and gardening can be fun and a great stress-reliever. The projects and techniques in this book aim to save you time and energy and give you a new perspective on the work that needs doing. Rushing around doing things the hard way is not the answer. The 20 minute theme does not mean you must spend that amount of time working in the garden, either daily or weekly. The aim is to get the garden under control and keep it that way. Sometimes, this means employing a professional to do a specific task – say, remove a tree – to save you time. Or, to create instant impact in a new or boring garden, it means buying specimen plants that are larger than normal ones. All the projects in this book can be achieved in about 20 minutes, but they can be expanded upon as well, and some can be done in stages. Enjoy your garden and with all the time you save you will be able to spend more than 20 minutes doing just that.

The right tools

Having the right tools and using them correctly can save an immense amount of time. It is not necessary to buy every tool on the market, but choose the best you can afford – stainless steel if possible. You will save time maintaining them and, of course, they will last much longer. However, do not overestimate the ability of each tool, as this will result in breakages. A nucleus of good tools will save money and time, but try to avoid buying gadgets if possible.

Dutch hoe. This is the most versatile one to choose.

Garden fork. Using a big one will speed up your digging.

Spring-tined wire rake, ideal for a variety of tasks.

Half-moon edger. Use this to neaten and redefine the edge of your lawn.

Border spade. Being smaller, this is easier to manage.

Long-handled lawn edging shears save you bending down.

Wheelbarrows and watering cans

Choose a good-sized wheelbarrow that is comfortable to handle. This one has a hardwearing polypropylene body and a large tyre that makes it easy to push. Store wheelbarrows and tools where they are protected from the weather. Watering cans should be easy to carry when full. Keep two in different colours, one for watering and one for poisonous chemicals.

Hand trowel. Choose a sturdy one for everyday use.

Hand cultivator. Ideal for weeding and breaking up the soil surface in small areas.

A basic tool kit

These tools will help you do most jobs around the garden: border spade, garden fork, hand fork, dutch hoe, loppers with telescopic handles, secateurs, trowel with planting depths marked on it, wire lawn rake, hedging shears, lawn edging shears, half-moon edger, daisy grubber, wheelbarrow and watering can.

Daisy grubber. Use this to lift lawn weeds without damaging the turf.

Hand fork, a basic tool for many tasks.

Loppers with extendable handles.

There are various hoes on the market, but the dutch hoe can do a variety of jobs including weeding, making drills and holes for sowing and planting and aerating the soil.

Secateurs. You can choose from a wide range of models to suit your needs.

Buy the best-quality secateurs possible, as it will be possible to obtain spare parts for them and there is usually a maintenance service. They will also cut better and for longer.

Use spring-tined rakes for scarifying lawns, collecting leaves and debris and for raking gravel.

Hedging shears. Use them for trimming and quick pruning of bushy plants.

Pruning saw. Use it on branches that are too large for secateurs and loppers to deal with comfortably.

TIME SAVING TECHNIQUES

Getting organised

As every busy person knows, if you want to save time, you must be organised. Try to manage the time you spend in the garden. Hang a shoe tidy in a convenient place as a garden organiser, so that all your tools and accessories are to hand in one place when you need them for those 20-minute tasks. You can pop notes into a pocket when a project comes to mind, and they will be a reminder when you go out into the garden. A pair of rubber overshoes in two pockets mean that even if the ground outside is wet, you won't waste time looking for suitable footwear. Gardening gloves help to keep your hands clean in the garden and avoid that scrabble to wipe dirty hands when the telephone rings. Other useful items include secateurs, a trowel, packets of seeds, a spot weeder, labels, marker pen or pencil, string, scissors, daisy grubber (useful for digging out the odd perennial weed), bug spray, slug/snail bait and a supply of plastic bags to collect weeds to put on the compost heap or to harvest fruit or herbs.

Left: A shoe tidy on the garden door can hold tools, garden shoes and all the other basic items you need when you have a few spare moments to work outdoors.

This handy carrier with drawers is another way of storing tools and accessories.

Control in a few minutes

You can keep your garden under control in a few minutes a day. Dealing with routine tasks, being aware that new weeds are sprouting and keeping a lookout for the slightest signs of pest infestation means you can take action to prevent a small problem becoming a major worry.

Deadheading

Deadheading a plant means removing any flowers that are past their best or have begun to set seed. In the case of annuals, this will encourage the plant to produce more flowers. In plants such as rhododendrons, removing the old flower heads helps the plant to put its energy into producing flower buds for the following season. Snap off the dead flowers of bulbs, particularly narcissi, leaving the foliage to die down naturally. In the six weeks between the flowers finishing and the foliage dying, the leaves manufacture the food for the flowers the following year. As you walk round the garden, nip off any fading flowers and drop them onto the compost heap.

Deadhead perennial geraniums with scissors to encourage them to produce another show of flowers. Trim them back almost to ground level and within weeks there will be a flush of fresh new growth, followed by a second flowering.

Weeds

Slice off annual weeds at ground level with a hoe. As long as they do not have any seed heads, you can leave them on the soil to dry out and die. Keep a touchweeder handy, to deal with perennial weeds in an instant.

General hints

Many perennials, such as *Sedum spectabile*, have an untidy growth habit, but there is no need to spend time constructing a support for them with string and canes. Instead, buy a support frame from the garden centre and place it over the plant in early spring. The plant will grow through the frame during the season and the foliage will hide the frame but still have all the support it needs.

At the first sign of aphids on a plant stem, run your forefinger and thumb up the stem and squash the pests. If there is a severe infestation of aphids or any other pests, spray them with a specifically formulated chemical. Spray in the evening to avoid scorching flowers and foliage and to avoid damaging beneficial insects, such as lacewings and ladybirds.

As leaves begin to fall on lawns, and if the weather is still dry and warm, mow the grass with a rotary mower with a box attached. The leaves will be chopped up and collected along with the grass clippings. As the weather becomes colder and wetter, you will have to rake the leaves by hand. For large areas, a lawn vacuum will speed up the process.

Some climbing plants need tying to their supports. Do this as they grow, while the stems are still soft and pliable. It is much easier at this stage than when the stem has become woody and unbending.

Below: If hanging or storage space is a problem, keep a lightweight clip-on belt handy with the basic tools you need to keep the garden tidy.

A holster belt for tools leaves your hands free.

Right: Remove the dead flowerheads of herbaceous plants, such as this aquilegia, before the seeds have fully ripened to prevent rampant self-seeding. Treat alliums (ornamental onions) and Alchemilla mollis *in the same way.*

Make time for compost

When time is short, you might wonder whether it is worthwhile establishing a compost heap and waiting for the results. However, making compost has plenty of advantages. To begin with, it is an excellent way of recycling all kinds of garden and household waste. Instead of creating unsightly piles of weeds and prunings in the corner of the garden or trying to cram them into bags that split or become very heavy, simply drop lawn clippings, shredded woody growth and annual weeds into the composter and save time disposing of them in bulk. Secondly, when used as a mulch and spread over beds and borders, compost helps to retain moisture and saves time on watering. But above all, compost improves the soil quality, and when incorporated into garden soil at planting time, gets your plants off to a good start and encourages strong growth.

Plastic-coated metal rod 1.2m (48in) long.

Plastic mesh 1m (39in) wide and 2m (78in) long.

Grass cuttings

Compost accelerator

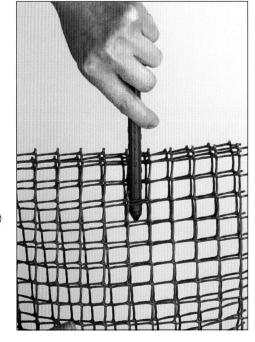

1 Select a level site on bare soil or on grass for the composter. First form a circle with the plastic mesh. Overlap the sides of the mesh by about 15-20cm (6-8in) and insert the rod through a hole at the top of the mesh. Weave the rod through the holes down to soil level. Push the rod firmly into the ground.

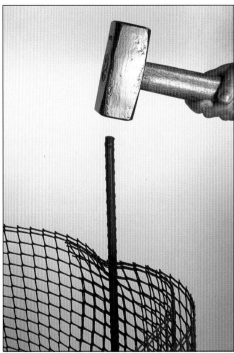

2 Using a small club hammer, carefully knock the plastic-coated metal rod into the ground until the top of the rod is just above the level of the mesh. If a larger composting area is required, you may need two or more rods. This composter will be used only for grass cuttings, but would work just as well with leaves or a mixture of suitable household and garden ingredients.

What to put on a compost heap

Grass cuttings, annual weeds, shredded newspaper, wool, animal hair, farmyard or horse manure, debris from vacuum cleaners, wood ash, vegetable peelings, chopped up citrus peelings, tea leaves and tea bags.

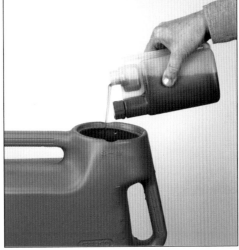

3 Place the grass cuttings evenly over the base of the composter and add more until the composter is about a quarter full. The fresher the cuttings, the greater the heat they will produce.

4 Select an activator that is suitable for the ingredients used in the compost heap. Dilute liquid activators in water. Pour the recommended dose into a watering can filled with water.

5 Thoroughly soak the surface of the grass cuttings using a watering can fitted with a fine spray rose. If you use a granular activator, scatter the granules evenly over the surface.

The key to success

You can build up a heap in a simple enclosure as shown here or buy a ready-made compost bin from a garden centre or hardware shops. The most important point to remember is to layer all the ingredients, as this will prevent the heap turning into a soggy mess. Adding an activator will speed up the process. There are activators for specific ingredients, including one for grass cuttings. This means that you can make a viable compost heap just using lawn mowings.

The ideal finished result – rich, crumbly compost for beds and borders.

6 Continue the layering process during the growing season until the composter is completely full. Water the contents in hot dry weather. To keep the compost moist, cover it with heavy duty black plastic or old carpet.

What not to put on a compost heap

Diseased plant material, roots of perennial weeds, coal ash, meat scraps (including bones), lumps of soil (particularly heavy clay), cardboard. Sticks, branches and rose clippings that have not been shredded, grass cuttings recently treated with chemicals. Only add straw bedding; bedding that contains shavings takes longer to rot down and if used when fresh can remove nitrogen from the soil.

Feed your plants

Plants that are fed are healthy plants, saving you time on spraying against disease, cutting off dead and dying branches or even having to remove dead plants completely and then replace them. There is a vast range of plant food to choose from, both organic and chemical. Organic feed tends to be bulky and storage may be difficult, but bonemeal, fish, blood and bone, and seaweed meal are available in small quantities. There is a wide choice of inorganic feeds in dry or liquid form. Feed only in the growing season and always use the appropriate food. Acid-loving plants must be given an ericaceous, or lime-free, feed. It is equally important not to overfeed, as this can also cause problems. Plants that are overfed may produce lush green growth and overfeeding may even stop the plant from producing flowers. Always follow the manufacturer's directions for dosage rates.

Left: Because hanging baskets need constant watering, any food quickly leaches away. The planting mix will incorporate a slow-release fertiliser, but basket plants will benefit from the extra boost of a high-potash food.

Below: You can choose from a wide variety of products designed to keep container plants looking good all season. The basic necessities are water-retaining crystals and slow-release feed granules. You can buy these separately or in combination.

Slow-release feed granules and gel crystals combined.

Slow-release feed in sachets. Insert unopened into the potting mix.

Slow-release feed in convenient pellet form.

Water-retaining gel crystals packed for single containers.

Your plants need food

Most plants benefit from feeding. On clay soils, an annual mulch in the autumn with well-rotted manure is probably all that is required. Sandy or chalky soils will need additional food formulated for shrubs and herbaceous plants. Begin feeding in spring with a slow-release fertiliser. In summer, use a quick-release food. Liquid feeds work more quickly than powdered ones. Do not feed in winter, as this will result in soft new growth that will be damaged by frost. Apply a slow-release feed when first planting alpines. They seldom need further feeding.

Right: Rhododendrons, pieris and conifers, all pictured here, are all lime-haters and must be given an ericaceous feed. It is easier to use a liquid feed for plants in containers.

Above: Conifers appreciate a general-purpose feed annually in spring, especially if they are planted in grassed areas. Sprinkle the granules onto the soil, avoiding the foliage.

Right: One of the simplest ways to feed your plants is with a hose end feeder. These are produced by various manufacturers. Fill the feeder with a powder or insert a tablet and then attach the feeder to the end of a hose.

Watering wisely

All plants need water to survive, especially in the first year of planting. It is important not to waste water, and for the busy person it is also important not to waste time watering. A rainwater butt is one of the easiest ways to collect water and is handy for borders and containers nearby, but not practical for watering further away. For this purpose, consider installing a computer-controlled watering system, using soaker hoses or a micro-drip set-up. Do not water well-established plants continuously, as this can discourage them from sending down deep tap roots to find their own water.

Supply tube. Large bore pipe that carries mains supply water from the timer to the irrigation setup.

Electronic water timer. Battery-powered device that turns the water on and off as programmed.

Pressure regulator. This reduces the mains water pressure to suit the system.

Micro-irrigation hose. Smaller bore pipe that carries water from the main tube to the sprinklers and jets.

Use this tool to make holes in the pipes for connections and outlets.

Main control valve and pipe connectors

1 An outdoor tap is a must when fitting a watering system. The electronic water timer fits onto the tap and can be set to water two or three times a day for varying lengths of time. The water regulator, which reduces the water pressure, connects the timer to the supply hose. Follow manufacturers' instructions on how to assess your water pressure.

Support stakes, spikes, drippers and microjets. These deliver water to the plants and soil.

Watering tips

Do not water in the heat of the day, but in the early morning or in the evening when the plants will benefit the most. An hour spent watering in the evening is worth more than two hours during the day.

Use as many water butts as you can. Stand two side by side, joined together with an overflow connector.

For summer planting, mix water-retaining crystals with the potting mixture. These are not suitable for use in winter, as the compost will become waterlogged in wet weather. For patio pots and other containers in summer, use self-watering pots. These are containers that have a water reservoir in the base.

Manufacturers now produce potting mixtures with a wetting agent incorporated into the mix. If the potting mix is allowed to get extremely dry, the wetting agent enables the soil to absorb water again quickly and easily.

When planting trees and shrubs, such as the conifer shown below, insert a length of old hosepipe – or even a large plastic bottle with the top removed and the bottom cut away – alongside the plant. When watering, slowly fill the pipe or bottle with water, which will go directly to the roots without evaporating.

Above: A soaker hose allows water to seep through its porous walls, while a micro-irrigation supply hose has mini sprinklers or drippers. To disguise the hoses in beds and borders, cover them with bark chippings, but remember where the hose is buried so that you do not damage it when hoeing.

2 Lay the supply hose around the required area and, using the installation tool, connect the micro-hose to the supply hose. Fit a dripper and spike and push these into the soil in the container.

3 Fit a mini-sprinkler close to moisture-loving hostas and ferns. If you mulch the bed to disguise the pipe, leave a small area free of chippings by each of the outlets to allow direct contact between the water and soil.

Controlling weeds

Weeds are the bane of every gardener's life, but people with a hectic lifestyle just do not have the time for endless hand weeding. Annual weeds are relatively easy to deal with and, as long as they are not allowed to set seed, can be controlled with mulches, weed block fabric and ground cover plants. The simple act of depriving annual weeds of light discourages them. Perennial weeds are more difficult to eradicate and this is where chemicals can be a tremendous help. There are basically two types of chemical treatments. One is absorbed through the leaves, so do not allow it to come into contact with the foliage of any plant you wish to keep. The chemical is taken through the foliage, down to the root system. Although it may look unsightly, leave the dying weed in the ground until the plant is completely dead, otherwise a part of the root will remain unaffected and will regrow. The alternative chemical way of killing weeds is to use a product that is absorbed via the soil. This is useful if you need to clear an area completely. Treat weeds in lawns with a granular or liquid lawn weedkiller. Persistent weeds, such as clover, will usually need more than one application. Lawn weedkillers are best used in spring or early summer.

Above: Use a touchweeder on tough weeds with leathery leaves in the lawn. This is a stick of solid weedkiller that can be used in the same way as the chemical gel. On stubborn weeds, you may need to repeat the treatment three weeks later.

Above: Couch grass is a perennial weed with creeping underground roots. It is often a problem amongst herbaceous plants. Paint each leaf with the chemical gel, which will be absorbed by the leaves, killing them without damaging any other plant. Wear rubber gloves to prevent contact between the gel and your skin.

Above: Long, tap-rooted, perennial weeds, such as dandelion, can be difficult to eradicate. In a gravel area you can dig them up, but you must remove every last bit of root. An effective way to remove the odd weed is to paint it with a chemical gel. Apply this to the leaves using the brush supplied. The weed leaves should begin to shrivel and die three or four days after application.

Left: Buttercup is a persistent weed in the lawn and will smother the grass. Use a granular lawn weed and feed. You can spread it by hand or with a wheeled spreader that will dispense at the correct rate when pushed along at a good, steady pace. Coloured granules make it easier to see which part of the lawn has already been treated.

Weeding tips

Annual weeds: The trick with annual weeds is to learn to identify them by their leaves, before they even begin to flower. Removing weeds at this stage prevents them from spreading literally thousands of seeds. Providing you remove annual weeds before they have set seed, they will make a useful addition to the compost heap.

Control annual weeds by mulching the ground with a thick layer of bark chippings, cocoa shell or even gravel and using ground cover plants, such as *Juniperus squamata* 'Blue Carpet', *Lamium maculatum* 'Beacon Silver' or *Euonymus fortunei*. Clear new beds of weeds and cover them with black plastic or a weed block fabric. Before covering the soil, make sure that it is thoroughly moist. Put new

Left: A thick layer of mulch, such as this cocoa shell, helps to suppress weed growth and also conserves moisture. Be sure to clear the entire area of all weeds before mulching.

ornamental plants into the ground through slits in the fabric and cover the whole area with a mulch. The fabric (or plastic) and organic mulch together help to keep plant roots cool in summer and warm in winter.

Perennial weeds: Perennial weeds, such as couch grass, bindweed or dandelions, can regrow from the smallest piece of root. If you are digging up perennial weeds, collect them in a plastic bag and when you have finished, burn the roots or take them to a waste management depot. Never put them on the compost heap.

Chemicals are probably the best answer to tough weeds. Those with strong, woody growth, such as brambles, should be cut back hard and sprayed thoroughly once the fresh new growth has appeared. To kill bindweed, train it up a cane, allow it plenty of growth and then douse it thoroughly with a systemic weedkiller.

Mare's-tail has narrow, waxy foliage that does not easily absorb weedkiller. Bruise the plant by lightly treading on it. This damages the surface of the foliage and enables the weedkiller to work. Persistent weeds will need more than one application.

Above: Hoe off and remove mature groundsel (Senecio vulgaris). Once you recognise the adult plant, you can quickly deal with emerging weeds.

Above: This is the juvenile growth of the same plant. This is the best stage to hoe it off because you can leave it on the surface to die away.

Controlling pests

Chemicals will have a place in the busy person's garden, but with care, you can restrict their use to a minimum, thus reducing their impact on friendly wildlife. Spray in the evenings to avoid scorching plant leaves and harming bees and other beneficial insects. Use specific rather than broad-spectrum chemicals. Systemic insecticides provide protection over a longer period against aphids and other sap-sucking pests that not only spread viral diseases, but can also severely disfigure foliage and flowers. The grubs of the vine weevil are difficult to destroy. New potting mediums are available that incorporate a chemical to control these pests. These mediums are particularly effective in containers. Once watered, the chemical remains active for about six months. Always keep chemicals securely locked away and dispose of them safely when the labels are no longer legible. For safety reasons, never transfer garden chemicals to household containers.

Slug pellets are the most effective way of controlling slugs and snails, and here we demonstrate how to make a simple slug trap that is inaccessible to birds and safe to use where pets are present.

Paving slab

Plastic seed tray.

Trowel

Shower-resistant slug pellets

1 Site the slug trap in the bed or border where slugs are a problem. Dig out a shallow hole in the soil, slightly larger than the plastic seed tray. Place the tray in the hole and make sure that it sits firmly in the base of the hole.

2 Using a trowel, fill in any gaps around the outside of the tray with soil to just below the rim. Use a good-quality, solid tray with drainage holes. If water cannot drain away, the pellets become soggy and useless.

3 Cover the base of the tray with the shower-resistant slug pellets. Use plenty of pellets, as only the slugs will be able to gain access. Pets, birds and mammals will be excluded.

4 Position the slab over the top of the tray. Cover the whole of the tray, except for a gap of 2cm (0.8in) at one end. This will allow the slugs to reach the pellets.

Organic alternatives

A beer trap will also kill slugs. Fill a glass jar with beer and sink it into the ground. Replace the beer every day.

Earwigs are very fond of chrysanthemum and dahlias, and will eat young leaves and spoil the petals. Loosely pack a plastic flowerpot with hay or straw and hang it upside down on a cane firmly pushed into the ground near susceptible plants. The earwigs will shelter in the pots during the day; tip out the contents every couple of days and dispose of them.

Encourage friendly creatures into the garden to feast on any pests. These include birds, shrews, hoverflies, ladybirds and hedgehogs, which are the greatest predator of slugs.

5 An attractively planted pot placed on top of the slab will not only disguise the trap, but will also be an extra deterrent to any animal attempting to reach the pellets. Planting a slug favourite close by will attract the slugs to the site of the trap. Remove and safely dispose of any slug bodies on a weekly basis.

Plants for your soil

The most important factor in a busy person's life is not to waste time. If you know whether your soil is acid, neutral or alkaline, you can select plants that will thrive in it with the minimum of attention. The easiest way to identify soil type is to buy a pH test kit. (The pH scale measures degree of acidity or alkalinity.) There are two kinds. One involves putting a small amount of soil in a tube with a little water and then matching the colour of the water to a card. There is also an electronic meter, which you push directly into the soil. The majority of plants do well in most soils, especially if the soil proves to be neutral. However if the soil is clearly acid or alkaline, it is most important to choose suitable plants; don't fight nature!

The second vital task is to improve the condition of the soil, unless of course you are lucky enough to have a loamy soil. If the soil is light, dig in masses of organic matter to improve soil fertility. If it is heavy, add grit to improve drainage. You can improve your soil gradually over a period of time; it doesn't mean hours of backbreaking work. As well as knowing what type of soil you have, consider the aspect of your garden. Is it sunny or shady? All soils and positions have their advantages and disadvantages. Having selected the right plant for the right spot and planted it, water it well for the first growing season.

Testing the pH of your soil

Plastic test container

Pipette to fill test chamber with water

Test colour chart

Chemical added to water to cause colour change

1 For best results, take a soil sample from 5-7.5cm (2-3in) below the surface, break it up and allow it to dry before carrying out the test.

2 Open one of the green capsules and pour the contents into the test chamber, then add some of the soil up to the line shown. Next, use the supplied pipette to fill the chamber with water up to the second line.

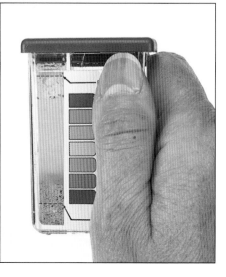

3 Put the cap on the test container and shake it vigorously to mix the soil and water together. Leave for a few minutes and compare the colour of the liquid with the chart. The yellow colour here shows that the soil sample is acid.

Plants for alkaline, or chalky, soil

The following plants will all tolerate a high-lime content in the soil and most positively prefer it alkaline. To improve the soil quality and texture, mulch annually with organic matter, such as compost or well-rotted farmyard manure.

Trees:

Celtis occidentalis
Cercis siliquastrum
Crataegus
Fagus
Prunus
Pyrus
Robinia

Hypericum calycinum

Shrubs for sun

Cotoneaster
Cistus
Elaeagnus angustifolia
Forsythia
Fremontodendron
Hibiscus syriacus
Hypericum
Olearia
Osmanthus
Philadelphus
Sambucus racemosa 'Tenuifolia'
Syringa
Viburnum plicatum 'Lanarth'
Weigela

Vinca minor

Shrubs for shade

Aucuba japonica
Euonymus
Fuchsia
Ilex
Ligustrum ovalifolium 'Aureum'
Mahonia aquifolium
Ruscus aculeatus
Sarcococca
Symphoricarpos
Vinca

Herbaceous perennials for sun

Acanthus
Achillea filipendula 'Gold Plate'
Aubrieta deltoides
Centranthus
Dianthus
Erysimum
Gypsophila
Heuchera
Pulsatilla vulgaris
Rudbeckia
Saponaria
Scabious
Silene
Verbascum

Herbaceous perennials for shade

Anemone
Campanula glomerata
Clematis recta
Convallaria
Dictamnus albus
    (syn. *D. fraxinella*)
Dryopteris affinis
Epimedium
Primula denticulata
Prunella
Viola

Tsuga canadensis 'Nana'

Conifers

Chamaecyparis lawsoniana
Juniperus
Taxus baccata
Tsuga canadensis

Climbers

Actinidia kolomikta
Akebia quinata
Clematis
Hydrangea petiolaris
Lonicera
Parthenocissus tricuspidata

Plants for acid soil

Even if the soil is very acid, there is a wide range of colours and textures in the plants listed below and many flower over a long season. Do not think that you will be restricted to rhododendrons!

Shrubs for sun

Acer japonicum
Berberis
Caragana arborescens
Cornus mas
Cotoneaster
Enkianthus campanulatus
Erica (summer-flowering)
Fothergilla
Genista
Kalmia latifolia
Leucothoe
Pieris japonica
Physocarpus
Tamarix

Lupins

Herbaceous perennials for sun

Corydalis
Geranium x *oxonianum* 'Claridge Druce'
Hemerocallis
Iris sibirica
Lupin
Lychnis
Molinia 'Variegata'
Phlox
Tricyrtis

Rhododendron

Shrubs for shade

Camellia
Corylopsis pauciflora
Crinodendron hookerianum (syn. *Tricuspidaria lanceolata*)
Daphne laureola
Enkianthus
Gaultheria shallon
Hydrangea serrata 'Bluebird'
Leucothoe walteri 'Rainbow'
Pieris
Rhododendron

Dicentra spectabilis

Herbaceous perennials for shade

Ajuga reptans
Alchemilla mollis
Athyrium filix-femina
Dicentra spectabilis
Kirengeshoma palmata
Liriope muscari
Phlox stolonifera
Smilacina racemosa
Uvularia

Liquidamber styraciflua 'Lane Roberts'

Trees

Betula (birch)
Liquidamber styraciflua
Magnolia 'Heaven Scent'
Nyssa sylvatica
Styrax japonica

Bulbs

Most bulbs will grow in acid soil, but allium and fritillaria do well.

Conifers

Abies koreana
Calocedrus decurrens
Cedrus 'Glauca Pendula'
Chamaecyparis
Pinus

Plants for clay soil

Clay soils are usually fertile but can be badly drained, so always add some grit when planting. The soil can also range from neutral to alkaline. All the plants listed will cope with heavy soil but may need extra watering in hot, dry weather.

Cotoneaster horizontalis

Spiraea japonica

Shrubs for sun
Amelanchier
Chaenomeles
Cornus alba 'Sibirica Variegata'
Eucalyptus gunnii
Laburnum
Lonicera fragrantissima
Philadelphus
Potentilla fruticosa
Spiraea
Weigela

Shrubs for shade
Choisya ternata
Corylus 'Purpurea'
Cotoneaster horizontalis
Deutzia
Escallonia
Ilex
Mahonia japonica
Osmanthus heterophyllus
Pyracantha
Viburnum davidii

Herbaceous perennials for sun
Helenium
Hemerocallis
Houttuynia
Inula
Lysimachia
Lythrum

Helleborus foetidus

Herbaceous perennials for shade
Aconitum
Aruncus
Astilbe
Doronicum
Filipendula
Helleborus
Persicaria bistorta
Polemonium
Rheum
Rodgersia pinnata

Plants for a hot, dry position

In a hot, dry spot, the plants will need to be well watered in the first year. Once established, they will thoroughly enjoy the conditions.

Shrubs
Artemisia
Buddleja
Ceanothus
Convolvulus cneorum,
Helianthemum
Lavandula
Phormium
Rosmarinus
Santolina
Thymus

Herbaceous perennials
Centaurea
Coreopsis
Echinops
Eryngium
Gaillardia
Kniphofia
Lychnis
Nepeta
Papaver
Sedum

Papaver orientale 'Helen Elisabeth'

25

TIME SAVING CHOICES

Busy people need easy plants

Avoid impulse buying and save hours on your plant selections by spending a little time at home choosing plants that suit your soil and situation. A few mature specimens will give immediate structure and impact to the garden. Fast-growing plants rarely know when to stop, so select less vigorous species. Remember that improved varieties of native plants will establish more easily than those that need special conditions. Make the most of container-grown plants; you can buy and plant them all year round.

Alpines

Mat- or cushion-forming plants need minimal care and are usually ever-green. Saxifrages, such as the one pictured below, are a good example. Several alpine varieties will grow in sunny or shady positions, but most require well-drained soil. Cut back trailing varieties after flowering.

Ajuga
Arabis
Aubrieta
Campanula carpatica
Erigeron karvinskianus
Geranium 'Ballerina'
Helianthemum
Saxifraga
Silene
Sisyrinchium bellum

Easy-care bedding

Buy colourful bedding plants ready-grown, or sow seeds directly into the ground. These often self-seed year after year. Pelargoniums (below) are excellent drought-resistant plants, available in upright or trailing forms.

Bidens ferulifolia
Centaurea (cornflower; direct sow)
Diascia
Godetia
Iberis (candytuft)
Limnanthes douglasii (poached egg plant; direct sow)
Matthiola longipetala (Matthiola bicornis) (night-scented stock)
Nigella (love-in-a-mist; direct sow)
Pelargonium (zonal and trailing geraniums)
*Senecio cineraria (*syn. *Cineraria maritima)* – silver leaf

Shrubs

Evergreens are available in a variety of shapes and colours and provide a focal point all year round. For a splash of colour in a shady spot, try *Juniperus* 'Blue Carpet' (pictured below). Select deciduous shrubs with a prolonged flowering period.

Abies koreana
Aucuba japonica
Berberis
Euonymus
Fuchsia
Juniperus 'Blue Carpet'
Mahonia japonica
Pyracantha
Spiraea
Viburnum bodnantense

Perennials

Bushy plants with a spreading habit are mostly maintenance-free. Cut them back hard in autumn. Choose with care and you can have colour in the garden from spring until autumn. Cut back *Geranium psilostemon* (below) after flowering; it may bloom again.

Alchemilla mollis
Anthemis 'E.C. Buxton'
Anemone japonica
Campanula persicifolia
Doronicum
Geranium
Hemerocallis 'Stella d'Oro'
Lamium 'White Nancy'
Nepeta faassenii
Polemonium

Bulbs

Dwarf bulbs are the most suitable for trouble-free gardening. Plant them under deciduous shrubs and their dying, untidy leaves will be covered in spring by fresh growth on the shrub's bare branches. Muscari (grape ivy, shown below) naturalises and spreads well. It has blue or white flowers.

Allium moly
Anemone blanda
Colchicum
Crocus
Cyclamen coum
Cyclamen hederifolium
Galanthus
Muscari
Narcissus (dwarf)
Tulipa (dwarf)

Trees

Unless you have a large garden, opt for slow-growing evergreens or trees that can be cut back once a year. Deciduous trees have spring flowers and good autumn colour. *Amelanchier lamarckii* (below) and *A. canadensis* produce white flowers in spring.

Amelanchier canadensis
Buddleja davidii
Crataegus
Eucalyptus gunnii
Gleditsia 'Sunburst'
Malus
Pinus mugo
Prunus subhirtella 'Autumnalis'
Sorbus
Taxus 'Fastigiata Aurea'

Herbs and vegetables

Most herbs and vegetables can be grown in a mixed border. Mint is best grown in a container, either plunged in the ground or free-standing, otherwise it spreads uncontrollably. Cut-and-come-again plants are the most useful and less likely to bolt. Both the leaves and stems of Swiss chard are edible. Ruby chard (right, sometimes called rhubarb chard) is the more decorative variety.

A selection of easy-grow herbs and vegetables

Chives
Mint
Parsley
Rosemary
Thyme
Courgette
Leek
Lettuce (leaf varieties, such as 'Salad Bowl')
Radish
Swiss chard

Choosing your plants

Some plants are wonderful, but require a lot of attention to keep them looking their best. Busy people won't have the time to deal with them, but do not despair – there is always an alternative. Other plants are best avoided because they are prone to insect attack. This does not mean you should avoid them at all costs, but that you should be aware of their drawbacks so that you can choose alternatives that will do the same job but with a lot less fuss. Here we look at some popular plants that might cause you time-consuming problems and offer some alternative suggestions.

Aconitum napellus

Poisonous plants

Bear in mind that some 'time-saving' plants may have other disadvantages; for example, they may be poisonous or cause skin irritation. This could clearly cause problems where children play or where pets might chew plants. It is worth bearing this in mind when buying plants, so always check plant labels or ask for advice. And teach children not to eat anything in the garden without asking first. Some common poisonous plants include: aconitum, arum, daphne, digitalis, euphorbia, gaultheria, laburnum, lupin, solanum and yew.

Hemerocallis 'Superlative'

Lilies

Lilies are wonderful plants, but in some areas are being devastated by the red Lily Beetle. The only really effective control is to search them out and crush them, a time-consuming affair. Lilies may also be fussy about soil and situation. However, the day lilies, *Hemerocallis* hybrids, are a wonderful alternative. They bloom all summer and are now available in an excellent range of colours.

Rosa moyesii with hips

Roses

Roses look wonderful in the border or as a cut flower. However, the hybrid tea (HT) and floribunda (cluster-flowered) types do insist on regular pruning and, if the growing conditions are not particularly good, spraying against disease and pests. Instead of a bed of these types of roses, use just one shrub rose. These are available in a variety of colours, heights and widths and can be used free-standing in beds and borders. Some can be trained against walls as climbers. Many shrub roses require minimal pruning and most not only have beautifully scented flowers, but are also followed by large orange-red hips. Suggested varieties: 'Cornelia', 'Ferdinand Pichard', 'Madame Isaac Pereire', 'Roseraie de l'Hay', *Rosa glauca* (syn. *rubrifolia*) and *Rosa moyesii* 'Geranium'.

Polystichum setiferum

Hostas

Hostas are marvellous in shady spots and can light up the darkest corner. Unfortunately, they are high on the list of favourite snacks for slugs and snails. This results in a very tired and tatty plant early on in the season. There are other plants that do equally well in difficult shady places. Ferns have the advantage of preferring shade and many are evergreen, too, which hostas are not. Some of the ornamental grasses will also grow in shade. Both ferns and grasses are far less likely to be worried by pests. For added variety, use ferns with different textures, such as *Asplenium scolopendrium, Dryopteris filix-mas, Osmunda regalis, Polypodium vulgare* and *Polystichum setiferum* Divisilobum Group. Other useful shade plants include *Helleborus niger, Lamium maculatum* and *Pachysandra terminalis*.

Note

The dreaded leylandii hedge is a menace in the garden. *Thuja plicata* is an equally good hedging plant, but less rampant and easily controlled.

Clematis montana

Clematis

Large-flowered clematis varieties are prone to clematis wilt, which can be very disappointing. It does not usually kill the plant entirely, especially if the clematis has been planted deeply, and the plant should regrow in time. However, species clematis very rarely succumb to the disease. They may have smaller flowers but there is still a good range of colours and flowering periods. Options include *Clematis alpina, C. macropetala, C. montana, C. rehderiana* and *C. tangutica*.

Hollyhocks

Hollyhocks can be prone to rust and will need spraying to keep them in good condition. An alternative is to use verbascum, which has a similar habit. These mostly have flowers in shades of yellow. *Verbascum nigrum* or *Verbascum* 'Gainsborough' will lend height to your planting scheme. The slightly shorter 'Helen Johnson' has salmon pink flowers and 'Mont Blanc' has white ones.

Pyrus salicifolia 'Pendula'

Trees

These days, many people have small gardens, where a large tree would not only look out of place, but could cause problems with its roots. Even a small tree may cast too much shade and you could find yourself lopping off branches to let in light, which is a waste of valuable time and can ruin the appearance of the tree. This does not mean that you should avoid trees altogether. It is possible to buy plants that have been grafted onto a stem to give the appearance of a small tree. They will grow a larger head in time, but the trunk will not get any taller. Varieties include: *Cotoneaster salicifolius* 'Pendulus', *Salix caprea* 'Kilmarnock' (Kilmarnock willow) and *Salix integra* 'Hakuro-nishiki'.

Reduce the height of trees such as *Pyrus salicifolia* 'Pendula' by cutting out the main leading shoot.

Apple trees need regular pruning. To avoid this, choose a Ballerina tree, which has a naturally columnar habit. Only Ballerina trees grow like this; others need to be pruned to shape.

A quick and simple path

If there is an area of lawn that has become worn with constant use, you will need some sort of path. The speedy way to create a pathway is to lay stepping stones. There is a range of styles to choose from, including preformed concrete circular slabs. You can buy or even make your own wooden ones, but these will become dangerously slippery in wet weather. They can be covered with wire mesh, but this is time-consuming and unsightly. The advantage of stepping stones is that you need only lay one at a time, which means you do not have to remove a whole section of the lawn to make a path. Using stepping stones also makes it easier to return the area to lawn in the future.

Border spade

Preformed concrete slabs

Sharp sand

1 Place the first stepping stone in position on the lawn and, with a sharp knife, cut through the turf into the soil all the way round the edge of the slab. Set aside the stone adjacent to the cut turf.

2 Following the cut shape, lever up the turf and remove it. Dig out the soil to at least 2.5cm (1in) more than the depth of the slab. Cut out any roots, as they may cause the stones to lift in time.

3 Cover the base of the hole with a thin layer of sharp sand and level off. This will ensure that the stepping stone is on an even, well-drained base and reduces the possibility of movement.

4 Replace the stone in the hole and push and twist it slightly to make sure it is firmly embedded. The stone should be just below the level of the turf to avoid damage to lawnmowers.

5 Do not worry if the stone does not fit the hole exactly; just fill in the gap by trickling soil around the edge. Firm down the soil with your fingertips. The grass will soon grow back and overlap the margins of the stones.

6 Before laying subsequent stepping stones, check the position and distance between each. A distance of just less than a stride is the most comfortable. A path that is not laid in a straight line results in a softer, more natural look.

Right: A path made up with old railway sleepers and gravel is easy and attractive, but will take longer than the allotted twenty minutes to complete.

Below: Square, imitation York stone slabs are as easy to lay as stepping stones. You can expand a path by laying adjacent slabs, as shown below.

Keeping the lawn in trim

Busy people want to keep their lawn in good condition without spending too much time attending to it. Keeping the lawn reasonably healthy and relatively weed-free makes it easier to care for. Fine lawns (those with very fine grasses) need a great deal of care and attention, so aim for a hard-wearing lawn (one with a certain amount of rye grass in the mixture) that is able to withstand some rough and tumble and is quick to recover from less than ideal conditions.

Lawn maintenance

To improve the lawn generally, spend the odd 20 minutes on maintenance. Aerate the lawn in autumn. Use a garden fork to make holes a few centimetres deep at intervals all over the lawn (for large areas hire an aerator from a garden machinery shop). This improves the drainage, particularly on heavy, clay soils. On light soils, brush fine peat or a peat substitute over the lawn after aerating to improve the condition of the soil and to encourage the soil to retain water, especially in summer. Finally, if the lawn is in extremely poor condition, employ a professional to remove the surface and returf the area.

Above: Use a garden fork to aerate small areas of lawn. Push the tines down into the soil to a depth of about 10cm (4in). Push the fork in straight and then lean it back slightly.

Left: Keeping the lawn edges straight makes mowing easier. Here, the one curved edge adds interest to the view. A relatively weed-free, easy-care lawn is possible without needing hours of care and attention.

Feeding

It may seem absurd to feed a lawn, only to cut it as soon as it grows, but feeding will encourage strong healthy growth, making it easier for the grass to overcome the competition from moss and weeds. Most hard-wearing lawns will only require a single feed annually. This is best given in the spring. However, lawns on light, sandy soils are an exception. Water drains away quickly on this type of soil, leaching any feed away with it. A liquid feed is the ideal solution. For small areas, use a watering can and for larger lawns, a hose end feeder. Other soils, especially clay, will retain the feed and only need a kick start in the spring with a granular, general purpose fertiliser.

If the lawn is particularly poor, there are granular products containing a fertiliser, plus a moss- and weedkiller that will deal with any problems. For small areas, spread them by hand using the dispenser provided by the manufacturer. For large areas, use a wheeled spreader (you can buy these or hire them on a daily basis). Liquid products are also available. Always follow the manufacturer's directions and do not be tempted to use a higher dosage, as this will only result in a burnt lawn.

Mowing

If the lawn is large, then a petrol-engined, rotary mower with a wide cut will make mowing an easy chore. An electric mower is easier to manoeuvre on small lawns. For the first cut of the year, use a box on the mower to collect the clippings. At this time of year, the grass will be longer than usual and is often damp. If the clippings are left on the lawn now, the new growth will have difficulty forcing its way through the sodden mass. Once the grass is being cut on a regular basis, you can remove the box from the mower. The fine clippings will be taken down into the soil by worms, effectively feeding the lawn. In mid-season when the weather may be very hot, cut less often, set the mower higher and reattach the mower box. Cutting the lawn too short during hot, dry weather can only result in parched brown patches, as there is not sufficient growth for rapid recovery. This in turn allows weeds and moss to take over.

Above: For small ornamental areas, use a mixture of the non-flowering, low-growing Chamaemelum nobile 'Treneague' and the mat-forming Thymus serpyllum. *However, this wonderfully scented lawn will not tolerate heavy use.*

Quick tip

If there is no time to mow the lawn, trim the edges. This will quickly make the lawn look neat.

Quick tip

Mowing takes time. If the lawn is tiny, you could replace the turf with gravel, but if you are determined to retain a patch of green, consider substituting the grass with one of the prostrate thymes. These will only need trimming back once a year after flowering.

Make mowing easier

It takes longer to mow a lawn with irregularly shaped flower beds cut into it. Make the beds square or rectangular or remove the plants, fill in the beds with soil and turf over them. To break up the expanse of green, place containers filled with permanent or seasonal plants around the lawn and remove them temporarily when mowing.

Dealing with moss

Never rake out moss from the lawn while it is green, as this will spread the living spores, thus increasing the problem. Apply a mosskiller or lawn sand in the spring, wait for the moss to turn black and then rake off the dead moss. Once you have removed the moss, feed the lawn, rake the soil where there are any bare patches and scatter some fresh grass seed. Moss thrives on poorly drained soil and in shade. Improve the growing conditions and the moss should decrease.

TIME SAVING TECHNIQUES

Gravel instead of grass

Many gardens have a small, often rather unhealthy, patch of lawn. This may be due to poor soil or a difficult site, such as a very hot or shady situation. Replacing the grass with gravel improves the area, which then needs only a minimum amount of care; just rake it occasionally to keep it level. Although removing the turf and soil will probably take more than 20 minutes, the process will save a huge amount of time in the long run. You can leave the gravelled area as it is or brighten it up by planting into it, placing a container on it or arranging larger stones or boulders on it for added interest.

Below: You can remove and replace worn flagstones with a gravel path. As the garden matures, the plants in the beds alongside will spill over the edges and self-seed into the gravel, softening the present, rather stark appearance.

Above: Create an attractive patio area by replacing grass with gravel and slabs. Combining containers with plants growing in the gravel can enhance a rather formal area. Employ a professional hard landscaper for a project of this size.

Left: An area around a seat can soon become quite worn. Instead of grass, cover the ground with gravel, pebbles and few larger stones. Dwarf aromatic plants in the gravel will release their fragrance when you step on them.

Creating a gravel area

1 A patch of lawn that consists mostly of weeds with bare soil showing through is the ideal spot for a transformation with gravel.

2 If the grass is overlapping an adjoining path or patio, make a neat edge with a spade. This makes it easier to remove the turf in sections.

3 Remove what turf there is and then excavate the soil to a depth of 5-7.5cm (2-3in) below the level of the hard surface that adjoins the area.

4 Make sure that the excavated area is fairly level. Wash the gravel and fill in the area with it. If you do not intend to plant into the gravel, lay down a membrane before adding the gravel. This will help to prevent perennial weed growth.

5 You can plant alpines or herbs that thrive in a well-drained site directly into the gravel. Choose plants that suit the site, whether sunny or shady. Self-seeding or mat-forming plants are excellent choices for this type of planting.

TIME SAVING TECHNIQUES

Pruning the quick way

The fastest way to prune is to avoid doing it at all. Some shrubs prefer not to be pruned and for gardeners with little time to spare these are the ideal choice. For a wider choice of plants, look for those that will only need pruning once a year. These can be divided into two groups: those that are cut back almost to ground level and those that have flowering stems cut out once the blooms are over. All plants will need tidying up at some stage. Cut back straggly stems, snip off frosted tips and remove dead wood. If you are not sure if a stem is dead or resting, scrape the surface with a fingernail. If the wood underneath is green or white, it should come back into leaf. If it is brown, it is dead and you should cut it back to green wood or to the base of the plant.

Loppers with extendable handles. Ideal for cutting stout woody stems.

Secateurs for cutting stems up to pencil thickness.

Hedging shears – excellent for quick pruning of heathers and similar plants.

Pruning saw for tackling thick tree branches.

Pruning buddleja

1 *Buddleja davidii* needs to be pruned hard in early spring. It is an extremely easy plant to prune as all the stems can be cut back to the same level. Begin at the outer edge and work towards the middle.

2 Prune down to 30-60cm (12-24in), just above a leaf bud. This promotes fresh, strong, healthy growth. Work across the plant, putting aside the branches as you go. Cut back dead wood to ground level.

3 A clean cut is essential. Do not leave ragged edges that would allow pests and diseases to enter. Always use pruners with sharp blades. These are anvil pruners, but those with a by-pass head are just as efficient.

Pruning strategy

Shrubs that prefer not to be pruned
Acer palmatum
Camellia
Cistus
Dwarf conifers
Daphne
Exochorda
Hamamelis
Hebe
Kalmia
Magnolia
Osmanthus
Pieris

Prune hard once a year
Buddleja davidii
Caryopteris x *clandonensis*
Colutea
Cornus alba 'Sibirica'
Cornus stolonifera 'Flaviramea'
Eucalyptus gunnii
Fuchsia
Perovskia
Rubus cockburnianus
Spiraea japonica

Prune while deadheading or cutting for the house
Kalmia latifolia
Rhododendron
Roses
Syringa
Viburnum tinus

Cut out old flowering stems
Brachyglottis 'Sunshine'
Deutzia
Forsythia
Kerria
Kolkwitzia amabilis
Philadelphus
Spiraea 'Arguta'
Weigela florida

Trim once a year with shears
Cerastium tomentosum
Calluna
Corydalis lutea
Cytisus
Erica
Heathers
Lavender
Mentha spicata
Santolina
Thymus vulgaris
Vinca

Right: Cut back heathers when they have finished flowering. Trim them with hedging shears to just below the old flowering head. Avoid cutting into the old wood.

Climbers
Lonicera (honeysuckle): When plants become a mass of stems, cut back to 38-50cm (15-20in) above ground level. Flowers may be lost for the first season after a drastic pruning, but the plant will be full of fresh new growth.
***Solanum jasminoides* and other slightly tender climbers:** Cut out frost-damaged shoots to keep them tidy.
Clematis: Choose varieties with care. If there is room, leave C. *montana* to spread and produce a stunning display in spring. Prune C. *viticella* annually, cutting back to a pair of strong buds at the base in late winter.

4 This treatment appears drastic, but a *Buddleja davidii* that is not pruned annually becomes straggly, with bare stems and fewer flowers. Pruning this way will produce a mass of blooms, enticing butterflies and other beneficial insects into the garden.

Left: A well-pruned buddleja will remain bushy and reward you with scented flowers from midsummer until early autumn. These plants are available in a range of colours, all of which will attract many species of butterflies.

Painless propagation

Propagation need not mean hours spent in the garden or greenhouse; some plants can even be propagated on the windowsill indoors. You can persuade many cuttings to root just by popping them into a jar of water. Fuchsia, pelargonium and impatiens cuttings will all root easily this way. You can also root some shrub cuttings directly into the ground. Forsythia is a good candidate, as are some rose species and most salix varieties. Another easy way to propagate is to allow annuals to set their own seed. If you do not deadhead some of the plants, the seedheads will ripen and the seed will fall to the ground, lying dormant over the winter ready to pop up the following spring. Some perennials, such as *Alchemilla mollis*, will also set seed this way. *Calendula officinalis* (pot marigold), *Centaurea cyanus* (cornflower) and *Nigella damascena* (love-in-a-mist) all self-seed very successfully. Propagate bulbs by digging them up after flowering, separating the clumps into singles and replanting them. Tulips, snowdrops, narcissi, crocus and hyacinth can all be propagated in this way.

Propagating fuchsias

2 Place the cutting on a flat, clean surface. Using a clean, sharp knife, make a cut straight across the stem just below a leaf joint. Remove the lower leaves to prevent rotting foliage fouling the water.

3 Put the prepared cutting into a water container, keeping the lower leaves clear of the water. This rack and the containers are manufactured specifically for use with cuttings.

1 Select a strong, healthy, non-flowering shoot. Cut above a leaf joint; this will encourage side shoots to sprout on the parent plant. It is better to take too long a cutting rather than one that is too short.

Propagating forsythia

1 In late spring, remove a non-flowering shoot from the parent plant using sharp secateurs. The stem should be firm at the base and soft at the top. Cuttings are best taken in the cool of early morning or evening.

2 Prepare a planting site in moist but well-drained soil, where the cutting can remain for a year. Make a clean cut straight across the stem just below a leaf joint. Remove the lower leaves and plant the cutting 7.5cm (3in) deep.

3 Remove the top soft part of the cutting to minimise moisture loss. The cutting will need some shade from hot summer sun. After a year, it will have sufficient roots for you to move it to its permanent position.

Cuttings of zonal pelargonium 'Madison'

Rooted fuchsia cutting

Dibber for making holes in the potting mixture

Multipurpose potting mix

4 Once the cutting has rooted well, remove it from the container. Fill a 9cm (3.5in) pot with potting mixture. Make a planting hole with a dibber, insert the cutting and firm in.

Propagating snowdrops

1 Spring bulbs are some of the easiest plants to propagate. Dig up large, overcrowded clumps as soon as they have finished flowering. Remove all weeds and grass from the clump before separating the bulbs.

2 Grasp the clump and, using a hand fork, tease out the bulbs into smaller bunches, loosening the soil from the roots. If the soil is very dry, soak the clump in a bucket of water without damaging the bulbs.

3 Inspect the bulbs closely and discard any damaged ones. Large bulbs should flower the following year, while smaller bulbs will take longer. Ideally, plant a mixture of mature and small bulbs.

Propagation by layering

1 You can propagate some shrubs and climbers by layering – literally by laying the stems down on the ground and allowing roots to form at a leaf joint. Select a pliable stem still attached to the parent plant, bend it over and push a leaf joint beneath the soil. You can remove the leaves with a sharp knife. Ideally, prepare the soil and add some sand for drainage.

2 Cover the leaf joint with soil and keep it in place by placing a stone on top. Water well and lay a further 15cm (6in) layer of soil over the site. Keep it moist through the summer and, depending on the plant, you can separate a rooted portion of stem 12-24 months later. The best time to start the layering process is between mid-spring and late summer.

5 Prepare fresh planting holes 5cm (2in) deep in the border or lawn and sprinkle a handful of slow-release fertiliser into the base. Snowdrops show themselves to better effect if replanted in groups rather than as single plants.

4 The original clump has been divided into four bunches of healthy stock ready for transplanting. Remove any seedheads that remain on the plants.

Galanthus nivalis
(snowdrops)

Above: An established plant of Alchemilla mollis (lady's mantle) in a container has self-seeded into the gravel alongside the pot. Lift the small plants out gently and replant them elsewhere – painless propagation in action.

Plants that you can propagate

By cuttings

Outdoors in the ground
Buddleja
Buxus
Cornus alba
Deutzia x *elegantissima*
Forsythia
Ligustrum
Ribes
Rosa (some species)
Sambucus
Weigela

Under cover in water
Fuchsia
Hedera
Impatiens
Pelargonium
Salix caprea
Salix tortuosa
Solenostemon (coleus)

By layering

Akebia
Clematis
Hedera
Humulus
Hydrangea
Lonicera

Rhododendron
Rubus
Vitis coignetiae
Wisteria

By division

Bulbs:
Allium
Crocosmia
Crocus
Daffodil
Gladioli
Hyacinth
Muscari
Nerine
Puschkinia scilloides
Tulip

Herbaceous plants:
Anemone hupehensis
Bergenia
Centaurea dealbata
Coreopsis
Doronicum
Geranium endressii
Helleborus orientalis
Hemerocallis
Iris
Sedum spectabile
Solidago

A stylish raised bed

Log roll is available in a range of sizes and is pretreated to prevent rotting. It is simple to assemble in any shape; use it to make a new feature or to raise an existing bed. It is ideal for easy maintenance and for growing plants such as rhododendrons if your soil is unsuitable.

Log roll 45cm (18in)-high

Pretreated cedar stakes (at least two)

Club hammer

Heavy duty black plastic

Trowel

Bark mulch

Soil-based potting mixture

Gravel

Aster novi-belgii

Hebe *hybrid 'Ritt'*

Trailing ivy Hedera helix 'Ester'

Perforated plastic pipe sealed at one end

Note

Join together as many log rolls as you need to make the bed the size and shape you require. Choose easy-care plants, but remember: planting is not part of the 20 minute strategy!

1 Form a shape with the log roll, making sure that the plastic loops at the end of each roll are lined up one above the other. Slide a wooden stake through the three pairs of loops.

2 Protecting the top of the stake with a piece of wood, drive it 30cm (12in) into the ground until it is flush with the top of the log roll. Repeat steps 1 and 2 with as many stakes as necessary.

3 For extra stability, put in some more stakes at regular intervals around the inside. Supporting the log roll with a piece of wood, secure the stakes to the roll with galvanised nails.

4 To protect the wood, loosely line the sides of the log roll with plastic. It can rest on the ground, but should not cover it. (You can staple the plastic to the wood if you wish.)

5 Neaten the edge of the plastic. Put a layer of gravel at the bottom of the bed, directly on the ground, to improve drainage. Fill up the bed with soil-based potting mix.

6 Lay a circle of perforated pipe on the surface. Attach the end of the pipe to a tap and water will flow out through the holes. Timing devices help to make the job even easier.

8 If the bed is viewed from the front, put the tallest plants at the back. If it is seen from all sides, place them in the centre, with shorter ones all round. Trailing plants soften the edge of the bed. Feed, water and deadhead plants regularly.

7 Position the plants in their pots on the bed to achieve the desired look. Soak the rootballs, remove the plants from their pots and plant them closely for instant impact. Water thoroughly.

Mulching the bed

You can mulch the bed when you plant it up or later on. It will improve moisture retention and suppress weeds. In this raised bed, it also helps to disguise the pipe. You can use a variety of mulching materials: chopped bark (shown here) and cocoa shells both look well with most plants. Gravel, available in a range of colours, is better for alpines; it prevents the plants rotting at the base.

A simple rose arch

A rose arch is an easy way of adding height and focus to the garden. Metal arches will last the longest and are available in a variety of styles, from a simple design in a galvanised metal finish to an ornate structure, which may be either galvanised, plastic-coated or painted. These are sold in kit form and are easily bolted together.

Rosa 'Climbing Mrs Sam McGredy'

Black, plastic-coated rose arch in kit form. Each side is made up of a curved section and two straight sections. The open-ended section goes into the ground.

Clematis viticella 'Little Nell'

Rose, tree and shrub planting mixture

Note

Constructing the arch will be a 20-minute project and the planting will take about the same time. If the arch is to be set up in a very exposed or windy site, concrete it into the ground.

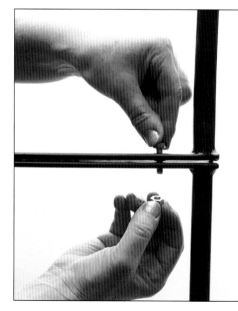

1 Lay the straight sections of each side of the arch on the ground. Join them together with the nuts, bolts and washers provided with the kit. Hand tighten them.

2 Measure the width of the arch and gently hammer in the open-ended section, protecting the finish with a piece of wood. Repeat the process on the other side at the correct distance.

3 On the outside of the arch, dig a hole for the clematis so that its rootball will lie 10cm (4in) below soil level. Add some planting mixture to the base of the hole.

4 Remove the clematis from its pot and place it in the hole. Fill in the hole with soil, adding more planting mix if the soil is poor. Gently firm in around the stems and water in well.

5 Repeat the procedure with the rose, but this time make sure that the final level of the soil is not above the point of the graft. The clematis needs to be deeper to protect its stems.

6 When planting a rose in early spring or late autumn, prune back to a healthy, outward facing shoot or bud, using sharp secateurs. Tie in both plants with twist ties as they grow.

Suitable plants

Roses are popular for training round arches. Climbing roses are more suitable than rambling roses, as ramblers are usually more vigorous and will become too heavy for the arch. To prolong the flowering season, plant an early- or late-flowering clematis with the rose. If the clematis is one of the viticella varieties, prune it back to about 90cm (36in) in the autumn, which makes it easier to control. Good companions include:

Rosa 'Golden Showers' with *Clematis tangutica* 'Bill MacKenzie'
Rosa 'Compassion' with *Clematis macropetala*
Rosa 'Climbing Mrs Sam McGredy' with *Clematis viticella* 'Little Nell'
Rosa 'Pink Perpétué' with *Clematis viticella* 'Ernest Markham'
Rosa 'High Hopes' with *Clematis* 'Perle d'Azur'

An all-white combination of climbing rose 'Iceberg' with *Clematis* 'Henryi' makes a stunning display for late spring and summer.

Left: *In summer, the rose arch provides instant height, scent and colour, and also creates a decorative frame to the view beyond. A series of arches, alternating roses with other climbers, could form a tunnel of fragrance.*

Right: *With its mass of rose stems, the arch is a focal point, even in the depths of winter. Hanging containers of food on the arch for the birds will bring movement and colour to the garden, even in the bleakest months.*

Adding instant height

If the garden beds or borders look rather unexciting, transform them instantly by adding height. This is very easy to do using a metal obelisk, available in a range of styles and heights; it does not even need to have plants around it to look decorative. A simple pyramid of bamboo canes planted with annuals will rapidly become a stunning focal point. Pyramids made from hazel and willow and ranging in height from 30cm to 2m (12-78in) are gaining in popularity. For instant height in any part of the garden, buy wooden or plastic tubs with a trellis frame already attached. Large tubs may even be fitted with castors, which makes moving the tub around the garden easier.

1 Push the obelisk firmly and evenly into the soil. If you intend planting annuals, put the obelisk in place first and plant around it. If you use it with a perennial climber, put the plant in first and place the obelisk over it.

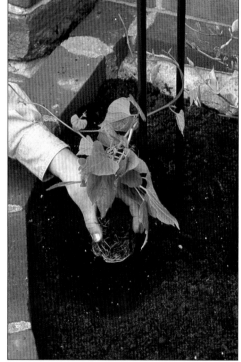

2 This is an annual climber, *Ipomoea tricolor* 'Heavenly Blue'. Select a plant with good top growth and a strong root system. Plant out annuals after all danger of frost is over.

3 Make a planting hole 5cm (2in) away from the obelisk and put in the ipomoea. Angle it slightly towards the support. Gently firm the soil to eliminate air pockets around the roots.

4 All climbing plants need a little help initially, even if they are self-twining. Use either plastic-coated wire ties or plant rings to encourage the plants to climb in the right direction.

5 When all the plants are in position, gently water them in. Thoroughly soak each rootball and the surrounding soil. Once the plants are well established, apply a high-potash food.

6 The obelisk is now covered with sky-blue ipomoea flowers that brighten up the plain stone and brick wall. Ipomoeas need a sunny position. Choose a different climber for a shady position.

Plants and combinations for climbing displays

Annuals are excellent for seasonal displays and also as a temporary stop-gap while you wait for a slowly establishing perennial climber to cover a wall or fence. Most climbing annuals need a sunny spot. Ipomoea is available in a range of colours, including white and red, as well as the traditional bright blue. *Lathyrus odorata* (sweet pea) also occurs in a rainbow of colours; choose those with a good scent, too. For something a little different, use plant combinations, such as a perennial climber or shrub with an annual, to add a splash of colour or scent. Possible combinations include: *Jasminum nudiflorum* (winter jasmine), with *Thunbergia alata* (black-eyed Susan, shown on the right), *Lonicera periclymenum* 'Serotina' (late Dutch honeysuckle) with *Lathyrus odorata*, or *Euonymus* 'Silver Queen' with *Tropaeolum majus* (climbing nasturtium).

An alpine sink garden

An alpine sink makes a neat alternative to a rockery, which can take time to maintain. Buy a cast concrete sink (available in various colours) or you may be lucky enough to find an old-fashioned butler's sink. Good drainage is essential, so place a good layer of crocks and grit in the bottom. Use a gritty, loam-based potting mixture unless you intend to grow lithospermum or some of the gentians, which require lime-free soil.

A selection of alpine plants. Aim for colour all year-round.

Crocks to cover the drainage hole

Fine grit

Loam-based potting mixture

Ornamental grit

Handy tip

Allow enough space between plants for them to grow without swamping each other. Cut back trailing plants after flowering to encourage fresh bushy growth.

1 Plant the main focus plant, here *Pinus mugo*, in a central position and work outwards with the remainder of your chosen alpines. This erodium is an excellent mat-forming plant that flowers through spring and summer.

2 Trailing plants, such as aubrieta, are best planted at the edges of the container. Planting the rootball at an angle encourages the plant to cascade over the side quickly.

3 Variegated evergreen alpines, such as this *Arabis fernandi-coburgi* 'Old Gold', not only add colour when in flower, but also brighten up the planting scheme on the dullest days.

4 When the plants have been watered in, add a layer of fine or ornamental grit. For something a little different, use the coloured gravel normally used in aquariums.

Dianthus 'Queen of Hearts'

Saxifraga 'Silver Cushion'

Euphorbia myrsinites

Pinus mugo 'Winter Gold'

Saxifraga 'Findling'

Armeria maritima

Aurinia saxatilis 'Goldkugel'

Sempervivum 'Royal Ruby'

Erodium reichardii rosea

Silene acaulis 'Mount Snowdon'

Aubrieta 'Oakington Lavender'

Arabis ferdinandi-coburgi 'Old Gold'

Saponaria ocymoides

Euphorbia myrsinites

TIME SAVING TECHNIQUES

Disguising eyesores

Most people have something in their garden that they consider to be an eyesore. It may be the compost heap, dustbins or oil tanks, or it may be that your garden is overlooked. Trellis is useful as a screen, easy to erect and available in various shapes and sizes. It can be left unplanted or used to support screening plants. Try to disguise the eyesore as naturally as possible. It may be something that only needs concealing during the milder times of year when you are sitting in the garden, in which case climbing annuals are the answer. If ugly walls are a problem, attach a framework of wires and train a wall shrub along them. Ceanothus is particularly effective on a sunny wall. Alternatively, use a self-clinging plant, such as *Parthenocissus tricuspidata* or *Hedera helix* 'Goldheart'. If you are overlooked by an ugly building, plant an evergreen to take your eye away from the view. *Ilex aquifolium* 'Silver Milkmaid' makes a particularly good specimen tree. Drain inspection covers can be unsightly in the lawn or on the patio. The problem here is that easy access is required, so do not cover them completely with plants. Plants grouped around the drain cover are effective and easy to move if necessary. The same applies to oil tanks, where access is essential.

Left: Use trellis and arches to disguise or separate off sections of the garden. Hang baskets filled with brightly coloured blooms – here tuberous begonias – on the trellis in summer.

Right: Even without climbing plants, trellis is useful for disguising eyesores, such as dustbins. Here, a small extension of the existing trelliswork was all that was needed. Hazel and willow hurdles are good alternatives.

1 Unsightly drainpipes are a common problem, but easy to hide with interlocking trellis designed for the purpose. Fix the trellis to the pipe with the straps supplied.

2 Use plastic-coated wire ties to attach the stems of a suitable plant to the trellis. This is *Jasminum officinale* in a container. Plants in pots allow easy access for maintenance.

3 Once established, the jasmine will scramble through the trellis. With several pots grouped around the base of the planted trellis, an eyesore has become an attractive feature.

Above: Here, evergreen pyracantha covers bare concrete walls. A mass of white spring flowers are followed in autumn by stunning berries, but it will take a few years to achieve this effect.

Right: A large water tank may be a necessity, but you can hide it with a climbing plant – here ivy. The covering of plants will also help to cool the water in summer.

Liven up a boring garden

It is tempting to think that a boring garden won't need much time-consuming attention, but it does not take long to add a few individual touches that will make it an inviting but still trouble-free place to enjoy. You may have moved into a new house with a bland plot laid out by contractors, or into a property with an established but uninspiring garden. The suggestions on these pages will help you to add some instant impact. If the garden is an established one, do not make any major changes for the first year, as there may be hidden treasures that will appear as the seasons come and go.

Instant colour

Buy pots of bulbs in flower and sink the whole pot into the ground. When they have finished flowering, replace them with others. Start the season with dwarf daffodils and snowdrops and progress through the summer with lilies, agapanthus and cannas.

A bird bath and feeding station in the garden will provide instant colour and added interest, as local birds are drawn to the food. Encouraging birds to the garden has other benefits, as they will also eat harmful insects.

For summer colour, stand groups of eye-catching pots in any position around the garden. Buy ready-planted flower arrangements from garden centres and slip them into decorative containers. Remove and dispose of the plants at the end of the season and replace them with winter interest.

Right: For instant colour in the winter, buy ready planted displays from garden centres. This pot features winter-flowering heather, Ilex 'Lawsoniana', cotoneaster and grey santolina.

It isn't necessary to spend hours changing the shape of a boring garden. Consider changing the shape of the lawn, instead; if it is rectangular, cutting the corners into interesting shapes will transform it.

Stand a large tub by the doorway and add a plant with brightly coloured foliage, such as *Phormium tenax* 'Dazzler', or a highly scented plant, such as *Lonicera* 'Graham Thomas'. A large *Photinia* x *fraseri* 'Red

Robin', with its young, bright red foliage and white summer flowers will add impact to the dullest garden.

A simple bench or seat can provide a fresh focal point from which to contemplate the garden from a different viewpoint. Stand a plant with aromatic foliage next to the seat to add to the pleasure.

To cheer up a boring bed or border, place a statue in it, plant a small-leaved ivy, such as *Hedera helix* 'Sagittifolia', at the base and twist the stems around the statue. Small-leaved ivy is less likely to swamp the statue.

An unusual container can provide a focal point in an instant. Use an obelisk with or without a climbing plant to give instant height.

Liven up a boring conifer needed for screening by growing a *Clematis alpina* through it for early flower and a *Clematis viticella* for a welcome display of blooms later in the year.

Left: Use bulbs in containers for movable colour. The pink double-flowered tulip 'Angélique' here is underplanted with dwarf wallflower 'Tom Thumb'. Avoid very tall tulips in tubs, as their heads may snap off in very windy weather.

Note

Once they have flowered and the foliage has died down, remove bulbs from containers and plant them in the garden. Use new bulbs for pots each year.

Left: Well-positioned statues make marvellous focal points. This classical subject looks perfectly at home in the shrubbery. Hide small animal statues under shrubs for children to find.

Below: These stunning blue pots – here positioned on a few decking panels – would liven up the most boring gardens. Drop in plastic pots of colourful plants for extra impact.

Below: Transform a blank wall by adding a mirror; ensure that you fix it securely. The edges of this mirror are decorated with mosaic patterns of shells, pebbles and tiles, and are softened by Hedera helix 'Goldheart', Polemonium caeruleum, Fatsia japonica *and* Ficus 'Brown Turkey'.

Quick topiary in a tub

Topiary can be used to great effect even in the smallest of gardens and is available ready-formed in a range of sizes, but it is more fun to create your own. The traditional plant to use is box *(Buxus sempervirens)*, but this is fairly slow-growing and usually expensive. As an alternative, try a small-leaved evergreen, such as *Lonicera nitida*, which benefits from regular trimming. The variety 'Baggesen's Gold' featured here has yellow new growth for added interest.

You can buy three-dimensional preformed wire shapes or just a simple outline. When choosing the frame, plant and container, keep an even balance between the topiary frame and the pot.

Preformed 3-D wire topiary shape

Glazed terracotta container

Lonicera nitida 'Baggesen's Gold'

Plastic-coated wire ties

Polystyrene pieces for drainage

Soil-based potting mixture

Quick tips

A plant with uneven growth may suggest a shape even before you choose a topiary frame. Using a container with a fun motif will attract the eye until the topiary shape is complete.

1 Place polystyrene pieces in the base of the container for extra drainage. In winter, it may be necessary to raise the container slightly using bricks or ornamental 'pot feet' to aid drainage.

2 Cover the drainage material with a soil-based potting mixture. This is better for shrubs, as it usually provides more food over a longer period and tends not to dry out quite as quickly.

3 Remove the plant from its pot and place it in the container so that the top of the rootball is just below the rim of the container. Fill in the gaps with potting mixture and firm down.

4 Separate the branches as much as possible and place the wire frame over the plant. Push the stem of the frame firmly into the soil, without damaging any of the plant.

5 Tie the stems evenly to the wire frame with plastic-covered twist ties. Thin-stemmed plants will need several stems wired to the same point to generate bushy growth.

6 Use scissors to cut off any unwanted stems and to encourage new growth. Tie in the leading tips to the wire frame as they grow.

7 Water the plant thoroughly. All you need do now is wait for the foliage to cover the frame and to continue trimming it to shape with scissors. Feed with a slow-release fertiliser to maintain steady growth.

8 A perfect chicken in a pot. Trim the plant on a regular basis to maintain the shape and to prevent bare woody stems developing. An alternative plant to use is *Hedera helix* 'Ivalace', a variety of ivy with wonderfully crinkly margins to the leaves.

55

A stunning container

The range of containers is vast; in terms of size, style and material, there is something to suit everyone. Faced with such a large choice, it is worth planning ahead. It is important to choose something that will complement your garden. A wooden barrel with cottage garden plants would not suit a formal garden, and a clipped shrub in a Versailles tub will look out of place in a wild garden. As a change, try planting up an 'amusing' container, such as a metal watering can that has developed holes, an old washtub or a coal scuttle. To give terracotta containers a new look, paint or stencil them at home.

Standard Viburnum tinus 'Eve Price'

Frost-resistant terracotta pot. Use as heavy a container as is practical to prevent it being blown over by strong winds and to deter thieves.

Retain the bamboo cane with plant ties to provide support for the stem

Ranunculus *'Accolade'*

Primula *hybrid*

1 Place a layer of crocks, broken terracotta pots or polystyrene pieces over the drainage holes in the base of the container to assist with drainage in the wetter seasons.

2 Measure the depth of the pot of the largest plant. Part-fill the container with a loam-based potting mixture that includes fertiliser. This will feed the plants for several months.

3 Remove the main plant from its nursery pot and place it into the container. Fill the container almost to the top with the potting mixture and firm around the rootball.

4 Remove the larger of the seasonal plants from their pots and space them around the edge of the container. Fill in the gaps around the plants with more planting mix.

Choose from the wide range of plants available as standards or train young plants yourself.

5 Finish the planting with the smaller seasonal plants. Push them well down with your fingertips. Remember that odd numbers of plants look better than even ones.

6 Water in thoroughly using a fine spray on the watering can or hose pipe to avoid displacing the plants or potting mix. The container may need watering twice a day in hot weather.

Alternative planting ideas

If you can transfer the container to a cool conservatory for the winter, use half-hardy plants such as a standard fuchsia or anisodontea to prolong the season even further. A conifer with a columnar shape will provide a focus throughout the year; brighten it up in summer with a climbing annual such as *Tropaeolum majus* (nasturtium). Group smaller pots around the base of the large container for added interest.

A summer hanging basket

Hanging baskets can really brighten up the house in summer, but watering can be a problem for people with busy lifestyles. Instead of the traditional wire basket lined with moss, select a deep, solid plastic basket with a water reservoir in the base. For baskets that will hang in full sun all day, choose drought-resistant plants such as pelargoniums, bidens, plectranthus and tagetes. They will also cascade over the sides and soon hide the basket from view.

Pelargonium peltatum 'Narina'

30cm (12in) plastic hanging basket

Lysimachia congestiflora 'Outback Sunset'

Hanging basket potting mixture

Zonal pelargonium 'Boogy'

Plectranthus forsteri 'Marginatus'

Bidens ferulifolia

Tagetes patula (French marigold)

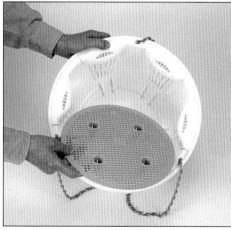

1 This basket has run-off channels that allow excess water to drain into the base of the basket below the drainage tray. Fit the tray before filling the basket with potting mix.

2 Almost fill the basket with hanging basket mix. This one incorporates a water-retaining gel and slow-release feed. Six weeks after planting, start feeding with a high-potash feed.

3 Plant outwards from the centre. Unless the basket will be hung very high, use a zonal pelargonium to add height, otherwise the planting scheme will look rather flat.

4 Plant three ivy-leaved pelargoniums (*Pelargonium peltatum*). Angle the trailing plants towards the edge of the hanging basket to encourage them to cascade over the side.

5 Place the bidens between the other trailing plants. Their feathery foliage and yellow flowers cascade over the side and thread their way through the other flowers and foliage.

6 Finally, slot in the tagetes (French marigold). Because these are grown in polystyrene strips, they have a smaller root system to begin with and are easy to fit into odd little gaps.

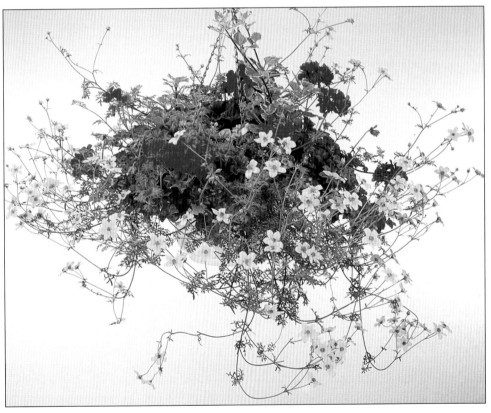

7 Water thoroughly. Hold the foliage aside to ensure that the water soaks into the soil. Before rewatering, push a fingertip under the surface of the soil to test how damp it still is.

8 The hanging basket should remain a blaze of colour throughout the summer. Remove dead flowers and feed on a regular basis to keep the plants healthy and blooming.

Plug plants and potted plants

Early in the season, most garden centres and nurseries sell plug plants (root cuttings). They are an inexpensive way of buying annuals and half-hardy plants for summer displays and are easy to plant into small or awkward containers. Alternatively, pot them into 9cm (3.5in) pots and grow them on until they can be planted out after the frost. Plug plants reach full size in four to six weeks, depending on the variety.

A basket for shade

There isn't always a sunny spot in which to hang a summer basket, so choose plants that will grow well in the shade and save time cutting back plants that have become long and straggly in their search for sunlight. One advantage of a shady position is that the potting mix won't dry out as quickly as it would in sun. White and pastel-coloured plants light up a shady corner and plants with coloured foliage add contrast. Plants that suit a shady basket include impatiens, *Lysimachia nummularia* 'Aurea', hedera and *Tolmiea menziesii*.

Some bedding plants for shade: Mimulus, Begonia semperflorens *'White Devil' and* Lobelia erinus *'Lilac Fountain'.*

Lined wicker hanging basket

Zonal pelargonium 'Glacis'

Fuchsia 'Holly's Beauty'

Sutera cordata 'Snowflake'

Helichrysum petiolare 'Limelight'

Plant feed and water-retaining granules

Peat-based potting mixture

1 Snip holes in the plastic lining of the basket for drainage. If the basket is to hang in the house or conservatory, leave the liner intact but avoid overwatering.

2 Add potting mix. When planted up, the soil level should be 2cm (0.8in) below the top of the liner. This stops the water running off the soil surface, allowing it to soak in thoroughly.

3 Add the feed and water granules according to the manufacturer's instructions. The dual-action granules provide feed for a season and help to retain moisture in the soil.

5 Continue to plant, radiating outwards. *Begonia semperflorens* 'White Devil' has wonderful purple-bronze leaves, as well as pretty white flowers. Unusual foliage colour adds interest to the basket while flowering plants may be resting.

6 Finish planting up the basket with the sutera. It produces a mass of small white flowers all season. The fuchsia used here is a California Dreamer variety with huge double blooms. Use as many plants as you can to create a stunning display.

4 Put the tallest plant in the centre. Zonal pelargoniums can cope with shade, although they may not bloom as profusely as in full sun. *Lobelia erinus* dries out less quickly in shade.

Watering and feeding

Water hanging baskets gently, especially when newly planted, to avoid displacing the soil and exposing the roots of the plants. Do not use a rose on a watering can or hose, as the water may simply slide off the leaves and not soak the potting mix at all. Sun shining on watered petals can burn and disfigure them. Six weeks after planting, begin feeding with a high-potash liquid feed once a week. This will encourage further flowers.

Above: After a few weeks, the plants are established and the basket can be seen in all its glory. To keep it looking its best, deadhead plants regularly and water and feed them well. They will bloom all summer.

A colourful windowbox

To save time, plant up the windowbox with a basic framework of perennial plants. These include dwarf conifers, hedera (ivy), heathers, dwarf narcissi, crocus and *Iris reticulata*. During the initial planting, use empty 9cm (3.5in) pots to create space for seasonal plants, such as pansies, petunias, fuchsias, geraniums and bidens. Slot the seasonal plants, in their pots with the bottoms cut out, into the holes made by the empty pots. This makes the change over from winter to summer bedding much easier and also means that you need not completely replant the windowbox every time.

A plastic trough that can be used on its own or slipped inside a wooden windowbox

Wooden windowbox treated with microporous gloss paint suitable for outdoor use

Chamaecyparis lawsoniana *'Fleckellwood'*

Osteospermum *'Sunny Yellow'*

Solenostemon *'Walter Turner' (coleus)*

Trailing lobelia

Tagetes *'Aurora Yellow Fire'*

Peat-based potting mixture

1 A plastic trough used as a liner in a wooden windowbox makes maintenance easier. Both trough and box should have drainage holes in the base. Fill the trough with potting mix.

2 The perennial plant provides the permanent framework, so set it in position first. We are using a slow-growing conifer with attractive foliage and have planted it in a central position. In larger containers you can use more perennials.

Useful tip

A simple way to make the change-over from summer to winter planting is to leave the plant in its original pot but to cut away the base before putting it in the windowbox. This makes removing the plant easy and prevents it from becoming rootbound.

3 You can plant annual bedding plants in their original growing pots, but remove perennials from their pots before planting them. Osteospermum may be used as a perennial or an annual. At this stage you can plant bulbs, which will pop up in spring to give early colour.

4 Coleus are excellent foliage bedding plants. To encourage bushiness and fresh leaf growth, remove the small flower buds as they appear. Coleus is not frost-hardy, but if you plant it in its original pot, you can lift it and replant it into a larger pot to enjoy as a houseplant.

5 Bedding plants sold in polystyrene strips have small root systems that are easy to fit into odd spaces. Trailing lobelia will cascade over the hard edge of the windowbox.

The colour of the trough should complement the plants.

6 Always aim for a balanced planting scheme, both in terms of the size of the plants and the colours. Too many different colours in a small container will appear messy and confusing – not colourful.

TIME SAVING TECHNIQUES

The overgrown garden

People with busy lifestyles may feel overwhelmed when first confronted with an overgrown garden. Where to start? How long will it take? The secret is to tackle the problem in stages. First remove all the obvious problem weeds, such as brambles and nettles. Cut them back in early summer and spray the fresh growth with a herbicide. If the lawn is overgrown, cut it back with a strimmer and remove the debris. This will give a clearer picture of the garden. Now you can stand back and take stock. An overgrown garden will really need a year without too much digging to give bulbs and herbaceous plants a chance to show themselves.

Above: Take cuttings from an overgrown forsythia before cutting it back almost to ground level. This makes a sprawling shrub more manageable if you want to remove it completely.

Left: If there are many overgrown shrubs in the garden, you may need to remove some of them completely and prune back others. Selecting which shrubs to dispose of will be a personal decision, but there is no point keeping something that is sparse of leaf or flower. Some shrubs, such as Buddleja davidii, *can be cut back almost to the ground, while others can be cut back in gradual stages.*

Above: Remove dead flowerheads and also suckers, which are young shoots growing around the base of a plant. Cut them away close to the roots of the main trunk, as they weaken the parent plant. Prune back overgrown bushes. This is a lilac (Syringa vulgaris). If you prune back an overgrown lilac to about 90cm (36in) it will become bushier, but may not flower again for two or three years.

General hints

Before drastically pruning or removing trees, you should check if they are covered by a preservation order. Dead trees will probably need to be removed professionally. There are two possible strategies: either cut the tree to the ground and dispose of the stump and roots using a stump grinder; or remove the top branches and seal the top of the stump with a pruning compound. You can then surround the trunk with wire netting and plant a climber against it, which will make an attractive feature. Seek expert advice on pruning overgrown fruit trees.

There may be an overgrown conifer near to the house. Most conifers will not tolerate hard pruning, the one exception being yew. The only option is to remove the conifer completely. Feed the soil in which the conifer has been growing before replanting.

Deciduous hedges that are out of control can be cut back quite hard, but this is best done in two stages, leaving a year in between.

Dig up herbaceous plants in the autumn and split them into sections. Replant the new growth and dispose of the old. Dig up bulbs after flowering. Split the clumps to make room for new growth and replant them.

Amongst the tangle of plants, you may come across straggly rose bushes. These are likely to be hybrid tea or floribunda roses. Unless you have a passion for roses, it is best to remove them (see Choosing your plants pages 28-29). Bear in mind that you should not plant new roses where old ones have been growing.

Right: Cow parsley (Anthriscus sylvestris) is a perennial weed, here growing through a large shrub rose. Pull out as much as possible before the flowers set seed. The only way to remove it entirely is to dig it up or to paint the fresh young spring growth with glyphosate. Do not treat the foliage of any plant you wish to keep.

Quick tip

It is very easy to dig up bulbs and perennial plants inadvertently while they are dormant. Mark the position of any plants you want to retain while they are in flower, so that you know exactly where they are.

Light up your garden

On those balmy summer evenings when you want to enjoy the garden after dusk, perhaps for a barbecue, you will need artificial light. Just one or two lights will make an instant impact. Discreetly placed low-voltage lights will enhance the garden and patio, creating a softer, more natural effect, while spotlights are useful for lighting up dark corners. A mass of tiny light bulbs in a tree or large shrub will produce a magical, even fairytale, look. White lights seem to work the best. Only use harsh floodlights for automatic security lighting. Use brighter lights in the foreground and dimmer ones in the background to give an impression of distance in a small area.

Above: Place a direct mains-voltage spotlight on a spike, in any position. Push the spike firmly into the ground and angle the head in any direction.

Right: Here, a spotlight enhances a statuette in her gloomy corner. The weatherproof cable runs along the wall base, under the bark mulch.

Left: This low-voltage downlighter has been used in the border to provide low-level lighting along the edge of a path. Downlighters can also be used to good effect alongside steps or to highlight a plant from above.

Note

Only use lamps intended for outdoor use. They should be waterproof, resistant to corrosion and able to withstand damp frost and snow. Make sure that all cablework etc. is installed by a qualified electrician.

Above: *Flares, which are like large candles, burn for approximately seven hours. Several of them together throw a romantic light on this seated area. Keep all candles and flares well out of the reach of children and pets.*

Below: *Hang a lantern on a hanging basket bracket. The soft light will enhance the foliage and flowers around it at night. A citronella candle will help to deter insects.*

Left: *Here, a low-voltage light has been used to good advantage under an ornamental grass. A slight breeze will give movement to the light. Take care when using lights this close to plants.*

A simple plant table

Sometimes you find yourself with an assortment of plants and pots and no obvious place to put them. With a bit of ingenuity, you can make a simple plant table on which to display these 'odds and ends' to advantage. You could even use it for a show of houseplants, such as succulents or cacti, that would enjoy the summer sun outdoors.

1 The plant table will need a firm base; a paving slab in a gravel area is ideal. Use house bricks that blend in with the colour of the paving slab as legs for the table top.

Note

This plant table has been created in its simplest form. An alternative is to use logs and a plank of wood. If you decide to treat the wood with preservative, avoid using creosote, as this will damage the plants.

2 Carefully position the 'table top' on the brick pedestal. This is an imitation stone slab. If the slab is heavy, it may need two people to lift it. Allow a slight overhang to the front and sides.

3 Stand a fairly tall plant, such as this *Coreopsis grandiflora* 'Early Sunrise' in its simple terracotta pot, centrally at the back of the table.

4 The golden foliage of *Fuchsia* 'Genii' echoes the yellow of the coreopsis. It will produce single flowers of red and purple until the onset of the first frosts during the autumn.

5 If time is short, drop the plants in their plastic pots into a decorative containers. Alternatively, plant them up, as here. We have used *Nepeta racemosa* and *Campanula* 'Blue Clips'.

6 Tweak the trailing stems of ivy (here *Hedera helix*) into the best position, so that they cover the edges of the container and the table.

7 As a finishing touch and to brighten up a group of plants, add some light-coloured flowers, such as this *Campanula* 'White Clips'.

8 By beginning at the back of the table and working forwards, and using pots of varying heights, the project has a layered appearance and the plants successfully hide the brick supports.

A *pebble water feature*

An easy-to-assemble pebble pool can give the garden a new image in just 20 minutes. Before choosing the site, remember that it will need to be situated close to a power outlet, as it will be used with a low-voltage fountain pump. (This uses a transformer to reduce the electrical power to safe levels.) Using this system, you can pop a child-safe water feature into a bare corner with very little effort. Placing the pebble pool into the soil is the fastest way to install it, but you could also set it up on a patio and surround it with interlocking bricks.

A selection of hardy ferns

Low-voltage pump

Plastic pebble pool base

Paddle stones

1 Measure the width and depth of the pebble pool base and dig a hole in the chosen site. If necessary, place sand in the bottom of the hole to keep the base level.

2 Position the pond with the lip resting on the soil surface. Lay a piece of wood and a spirit level on top of the pond to check that the pond is absolutely level.

3 Place the low-voltage pump centrally in the base of the pond. Always use a power circuit breaker. You will see that there is a notch in the lip to guide the waterproof cable.

4 Gently fill the pond with water. The level of the water should be just trickling out into the lip and the extension pipe on the pump must be above the surface of the water.

5 Place the cover over the pump extension pipe, onto the base. Lock it into position. Check that the cable is not trapped. Run the pump to check that everything is working.

6 Turn off the pump and cover the surface with the paddle stones or round cobble stones of various sizes. Gravel is not suitable as it will fall through and block the pond.

7 The 20 minute project is now complete, but to soften the edges add some hardy ferns. This *Polystichum polyblepharum* has been positioned to allow the fronds to trail over the pebbles.

Ferns in the display

Dryopteris affinis 'Cristata'
Dryopteris erythrosora
   (copper shield fern)
Polystichum polyblepharum
Dryopteris affinis (scaly
   male fern)
Dryopteris dilatata (syn.
   austriaca) 'Crispa
      Whiteside' (buckler fern)

8 The pebble pond, complete with the hardy ferns planted around it, now looks as if it has been in place for a long time. A bell fountain head fitted to the pump softens the flow of water, but still allows a pleasant sound of running water. Ferns will appreciate a semi-shady position; in a sunny spot use dwarf, ornamental grasses.

A pond in a trough

Using a water feature in the garden is the easy way to create the tranquil sound of running water without building a pond. You will find a variety of ready-made water features in garden and aquatic centres. There are tiny ones that can be used in the home and much larger ones that may include a fountain. For the 20-minute gardener, the best option is one that comes somewhere in between. A fairly basic feature is easy to change around. If there are small children in the family, fill the pool almost to the top with pebbles to avoid any risk of drowning. You can add plants, but unless they are very hardy marginals, remove them before the onset of frosts if the pool is very shallow. Also remove the pump and store it away in winter.

1 A water feature such as this will need a small submersible pump to circulate the water, which would otherwise become stagnant. Attach a length of flexible pipe to the pump. Do not cut the pipe too short at first. Remember to set the water feature close to a power socket and use a power breaker.

2 Stand the trough in its final position. Set the pump securely in the trough and cover it with pebbles. These are available in a range of colours and shapes; choose those that blend with the colour of the trough or container. Rinse them well before use to remove any dust or dirt.

3 Push the other end of the flexible pipe onto the inlet pipe of a stone ornament, here a frog. A small ornament is best in this situation, because if it is too tall any wind will blow the water away from the trough.

Suitable plants

Acorus gramineus 'Variegatus', Calla palustris, Cotula coronopifolia, Myosotis scorpioides, Typha minima, Veronica beccabunga

4 Sit the frog firmly and evenly on top of the pebbles that are concealing the pump. Cut the flexible pipe shorter if necessary. If you are using an animal ornament, try to set it in as natural a pose as possible.

5 Slowly fill the trough with water to avoid dislodging the pebbles. Switch on the pump and adjust the water flow so that it is not too fierce. You will need to remove the frog and a pebble or two to reach the pump.

Caltha palustris 'Flore Pleno'

6 Complete the water feature by adding some marginal water plants. Both of the plants used here can be removed and planted in moist soil for the winter.

Phalaris arundinacea var. *picta*

Alternative ideas

Instead of allowing water to circulate through an ornament in the trough, fix a mask to a wall above so that the water cascades down. Place a feature like this in a sheltered site protected from the wind. Keep the distance between the wall feature and the trough to a minimum to avoid splashing. Group plants in pots around the trough to soften the outline until the stoneware has weathered.

Handy herb pots

For maximum convenience with minimum effort, grow culinary herbs near the kitchen door. The traditional herb container with planting pockets can be difficult to plant and maintain, so use one large pot with a variety of plants or several small pots with individual plants. Another advantage of using small pots is that you can stand them on a sunny windowsill indoors in winter, thus prolonging the availability of fresh herbs.

Rosmarinus officinalis
'Miss Jessopp's Upright'

Thymus vulgaris
(thyme)

Foeniculum vulgare
(fennel)

Origanum vulgare
(oregano)

Mentha suaveolens *'Variegata'*
(pineapple mint)

Mentha spicata
(garden mint)

Terracotta pots

Petroselinum crispum
var. neapolitanum
(French parsley)

Loam-based
potting mixture

Suitable plants

Basil, chives, coriander, dill, mint, parsley, sage, tarragon and thyme will all grow in pots. The alpine strawberry 'Temptation' will grow in pots or hanging baskets.

1 Cover the drainage holes with a good layer of crocks and fill the container with a loam-based potting mix. It dries out less quickly than a peat-based one.

2 Plant large pots with hardy herbs that need not be moved inside for the winter. Make a good-sized hole towards the back of the container for tall plants such as this rosemary.

3 Garden mint is extremely invasive. To help restrict its growth, leave it in its original container but remove the base of the pot by cutting around the bottom edge with scissors.

4 Plant the mint, still in the original pot, deep enough to cover the rim of the pot. Complete the planting with herbs of your choice, leaving room for growth. Water in thoroughly.

Above: Herb pots look very effective when grouped together. They will brighten up a patio and are within easy reach when needed for cooking. If the herbs are not cut regularly for culinary use, trim them back occasionally with scissors.

Handy tips

In winter, when pots may become waterlogged, use decorative pot feet or bricks to raise containers slightly above ground level to aid drainage. Pot feet are available from garden centres.

When planting herbs singly into small pots, be sure to push the soil firmly down around the sides of the pot. This avoids air pockets forming, which harm root growth.

Succulent strawberries

Busy people do not have time to cultivate a large strawberry patch, but that does not mean you cannot enjoy delicious home-grown fruits, as strawberries are easy to grow in pots. However, you will need to protect the pots from wildlife; slugs, birds and squirrels seem to like strawberries as much as we do. The varieties 'Aromel' and 'Mara des Bois' are perpetual fruiting, but you can also extend the fruiting period by using varieties that fruit in different seasons.

Frost-resistant terracotta pot

Strawberry 'Elsanta'

Soil-based potting mixture

Terracotta crocks

Strawberry 'Red Gauntlet'

Strawberry 'Emily'

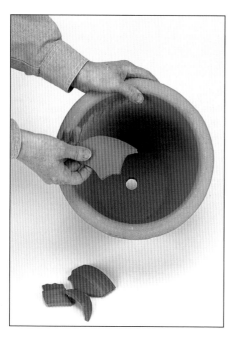

1 Select a container with one large or several small holes in the base and cover the holes with crocks. This will prevent the holes from becoming clogged with soil. Strawberries appreciate moist, fertile, but well-drained potting mix. Fill the pot with potting mix.

2 Use a trowel to make a planting hole. Plant the strawberry and firm the potting mixture around the rootball, making sure that the crown remains above the level of the mix. 'Red Gauntlet', shown here, fruits mid-season and will sometimes fruit again in autumn.

3 Plant 'Elsanta', which fruits in mid-season, and then add the third strawberry, 'Emily'. It is one of the earliest fruiting varieties and may need to be protected from frost to fruit successfully.

4 Water in all the plants thoroughly. Stand the pot in a sunny position and pay special attention to watering once the plants have flowered, as this will encourage good-sized fruits.

Note

Although it is best to remove most of the runners, you can peg down one runner from each plant into a small pot of soil to make new plants for the following season. Once the new plants have rooted and are actively growing, separate them from the parent plant.

5 The strawberry pot has now produced a good crop of succulent fruits that should continue throughout the summer. To strengthen the plants, remove any runners as they appear.

Protecting the fruit

Even if strawberries are grown close to the house, there will always be a cheeky bird ready to steal them just before they have ripened fully. Fine fruit netting is the only answer. Encircle the pot with the plastic netting and fasten it with wire ties. Place stones on the base of the netting to keep it in place.

Runner beans in a pot

Busy people who would like to be able to pick fresh, young runner beans from the garden without digging large trenches and erect metres of string and post, can grow them in pots. Seed merchants have produced a dwarf runner bean called 'Hestia' that is ideal for containers. Growing the beans in a pot close to the kitchen door means that it will only take a moment to pick some for supper.

Bamboo canes

A deep container is essential to allow for sufficient watering. This one is plastic, but any material is suitable.

Handy tip

If you have trouble getting the plants to produce beans, plant three or four sweet pea plants (Lathyrus odorata) in the same container. When the sweet peas flower, they encourage bees to pollinate the runner bean flowers, too.

Twist ties

Loam-based potting mixture

Runner bean seeds. This is the dwarf stringless bean 'Hestia'

1 Plastic containers may need extra drainage holes drilled through the base. Fill the pot with a loam-based potting mixture that has a high fertiliser content or use a peat-based mixture that is specifically formulated for growing vegetables.

2 Insert canes into the mix and push each one right down to the base of the container. Space the canes evenly around the edge. The shape of this pot makes it easy to assess how many are needed. Use too many canes rather than too few.

Runner beans

The dwarf runner bean is an excellent choice for patio pots, but other plants will do equally well. For something a little different try the dwarf mangetout or a variety of dwarf French bean with purple pods. You can also grow outdoor cucumbers in this way.

The first crops will be ready to pick after 8-10 weeks.

3 Pull the tops of the canes together and fasten them tightly with plastic covered wire. You can also buy plastic discs with holes in that will form a pyramid with six or seven canes.

4 Use a dibber to make a hole on either side of each cane about 3.75cm (1.5in deep) and pop in one seed per hole. If both seeds germinate, pull out the weaker seedling.

5 Once the runner beans are in flower, it is important to keep the pot well watered and fed with a high-potash feed. This will ensure a good crop of tender beans. This variety grows 45-60cm (18-24in) tall and simply needs to be tied to the canes to keep the pot tidy.

Tomatoes and marigolds

Home-grown tomatoes have a wonderful flavour, and an easy way to enjoy the taste of fresh-picked fruit is to grow a tomato plant in a hanging basket. There is no need to stake the plant, to support it or to take out the side shoots – simplicity itself. Just fill the basket with a peat-based potting mix for growing vegetables, hang it in a sunny position, water it regularly and evenly and feed it when the first fruits have formed. Use a food specifically formulated for tomatoes.

Tomato food

30cm (12in) hanging basket with reservoir

Tomato 'Tumbler'

Peat-based potting mixture

Tagetes patula (French marigold)

Note

Irregular watering creates problems. Tomatoes prefer evenly moist soil. Drying out and then flooding with water will result in split fruit or blossom end rot. The critical period is when the fruit begins to set.

1 Fit the drainage tray into the bottom of the hanging basket. This allows the roots to take up as much water as they need without the soil becoming waterlogged and sour.

2 Fill the basket to just below the overflow holes. Make sure the basket is fitted with metal chains; plastic chains may snap under the weight of the fruit-laden plant.

3 Using a trowel, make a planting hole in the centre of the basket. Plant the single tomato plant and gently firm in the potting mix around the rootball with your fingertips.

4 Marigolds are a good, natural deterrent to pests that are normally attracted to tomato plants, particularly whitefly. French marigolds do not grow too tall.

5 Three marigolds will be sufficient for this size of hanging basket. Plant the marigolds close to the edge of the basket to avoid damaging the rootball of the tomato plant.

6 Water in the plants gently but thoroughly. With this type of hanging basket, pour in enough water to soak the soil and then overflow down the channels and into the base.

7 To keep the basket healthy and full of fruit, include a liquid feed at every other watering. Pick the ripe tomatoes regularly. When the temperature begins to drop – and especially if there is a danger of frost – remove both red and green tomatoes from the plant and store them in a drawer. Including a few red fruits will encourage the green ones to ripen.

Suitable plants

'Tumbler' is the most reliable variety of naturally trailing tomatoes. There are other dwarf, bush varieties of tomato that will grow happily in pots. They only need regular watering and feeding, with no laborious pinching out of side shoots, and will produce an excellent crop of sweet, tasty tomatoes. Varieties include 'Red Robin', 'Tornado' and 'Totem'.

Speedy salads

Tasty, fresh salad crops can be grown at home, even when there is little time to spare. Grow them in pots in a sunny position close to the house and provide ample water and a good feeding regime. This way, the crops are close by when needed and there won't be too many at one time. A succession of sowings will provide fresh crops all season. Seed manufacturers now breed many more baby vegetables and these can be harvested quickly while they are young and sweet. Always select dwarf or small varieties or 'cut-and-come-again' types, particularly lettuce. Dividing the container into sections means that as one crop finishes, you can sow more seed for a later crop and still have produce to harvest. Once the plants are established, feed them weekly with a weak liquid tomato food. Wide, shallow plastic containers are excellent for salad crops, but keep them well-watered, as shallow pots dry out faster than deep ones.

45cm (18in) diameter plastic container

Peat-based potting mixture

'Little Gem' lettuce plants

Dibber

A selection of salad seeds

1 Fill the container with good-quality peat-based potting mix. For an almost instant crop, buy small lettuce plants from a garden centre or nursery and plant up one half of the container with these young plants. Use a dibber to make the planting holes and space the plants 10cm (4in) apart.

Suitable plants

Small beetroot, corn salad, land/ American cress, lettuce – 'Tom Thumb', 'Little Gem', leaf varieties 'Salad Bowl' or 'Lollo Rossa' – radish, rocket, spring onion.

2 In the other half of the container, mark out two lines in the mix about 15cm (6in) apart. Sprinkle lettuce seeds sparsely along the drills and cover them lightly with potting mixture. Label the seeds if you use different varieties.

3 Water in both the young plants and the newly sown seed. Stand the pot on the patio or near the kitchen door and just wait for them to grow. You may need to protect the crops with slug pellets.

Tender plants

Growing salads in pots does help to reduce the problem of weeds and soil pests, but aphids and slugs may still affect the plants. Use pet-friendly slug bait and a soap-based spray for the aphids. In hot weather, place the salad pots in a semi-shady position, as lettuce plants will bolt (run to seed) if the weather is too hot. Do not neglect to feed and water the plants regularly.

4 The lettuce plants are ready to harvest as soon as they have hearted up. Pull up the whole plant and then cut off the root.

The 'Little Gem' lettuces are ready to eat when they have reached this stage.

Left: As soon as you have harvested the first lettuce, dig over the soil with a hand fork and plant new seed. When the seedlings have produced a second set of leaves, thin them out, which means pulling out the excess plants. Thinning out gives the remaining plants space to expand and grow. By this method you will ensure a continuous supply of fresh salads.

Cut lettuce leaves grown from seed as soon as they are large enough.

Speedy vegetables

Salad crops and vegetables are extremely easy to grow in containers. Seeds marketed as 'baby vegetables' are the quickest to mature, so you will not have to wait for months before harvesting them. Sowing the seeds only takes minutes, and apart from watering them well and thinning them out, there is very little to do. Just wait a few weeks and then enjoy the crop.

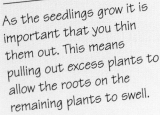

Note

As the seedlings grow it is important that you thin them out. This means pulling out excess plants to allow the roots on the remaining plants to swell.

Round-rooted carrot 'Parmex'

Spring onion 'White Lisbon'

Radish 'Sparkler'

1 Mark out three planting areas in the second plastic container filled with peat-based potting mixture. Label each section and sow the seed. We are sowing dwarf carrots, radishes and spring onions. Lightly cover the seeds with potting mixture and water them in.

2 Pull out excess seedlings at an early stage to give the remaining plants room to grow and thrive. Radishes are usually the first to be ready. As soon as you have harvested the first crop, sow some more seed. The spring onions and carrots will take a few more weeks to mature.

3 Approximately three weeks after harvesting the radishes, the spring onions and ball-rooted carrots are ready to pull. The round-rooted carrots are the easiest variety to grow in containers. They do not need the same depth of soil as traditional carrots, but are just as tasty.

Left: *All these plants were bought as young plants from a garden centre and grown in containers on the patio. Pot on the young plants into larger containers and keep them well watered. As soon as flowers appear, begin to feed with a proprietary vegetable food. Train cucumber plants up a tripod of bamboo canes. You can grow and harvest a good crop of slightly unusual vegetables with the minimum of time and effort.*

Aubergine 'Ova' produces white fruits. Vegetable crops can make a colourful and attractive display, as well as being edible.

Chilli pepper 'Apache'

Marrow (vegetable spaghetti) 'Tivoli'

Outdoor cucumber 'Burpless'

Courgette 'Gold Dust'

Note

All the plants featured on this page have certain basic requirements if they are to succeed. They need sunshine, water, a liquid feed formulated for vegetables and shelter from cold winds. Harvest the crops before the first frosts of the year.

Right: *As soon as courgettes have grown to about 15cm (6in), cut them from the plant with a sharp knife. They are much sweeter when harvested young and it will encourage the plant to produce more.*

TIME SAVING CHOICES

The family garden

Busy people with children have even less time to spare for the garden. Plant time-saving shrubberies and to save wear and tear on the whole garden, set aside part of it for the children's use. Encourage them to take an interest in the garden by giving them their own plots to cultivate and having competitions to see who can grow the tallest sunflower, the biggest pumpkin or the longest runner bean. Make a play area, too. If there are swings or other play equipment in the garden, place a generous layer of chipped bark underneath to prevent wear and tear on the lawn.

Making a play area need not waste precious time. Create an instant play pit with suitable sand and a plastic potting tray. Play pit sand is produced commercially and available in bags from garden centres. When the sand is not in use, simply tip it back into the bag, which will keep it clean and dry.

The family apple tree is a good choice for the busy family that would like some fruit in the garden. This has three or more varieties grafted onto the one stem, which means you do not need two or more trees for pollination. And you get crops of fruit that ripen at different times during the season.

Below: You can buy gardening tools for children. Very young children will enjoy playing with the pots and watering can, while slightly older children can use the mini rake and hoe.

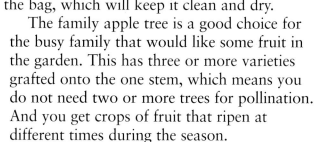

Plastic potting tray with rounded edges filled with play pit sand.

Above: Position a swing in a corner of the garden where, if the lawn becomes scuffed, it will not become an eyesore. Avoid planting prickly plants close to the swing and check all fittings annually.

Right: *The family garden need not look like a battlefield. High, well-kept hedges will keep footballs in your garden, not in the neighbour's. Tough grasses in the lawn will recover more quickly and resilient shrubs will survive the roughest play. The garden can look good and still be a playground for children.*

Suitable plants for the family garden

Aucuba japonica
Buddleja davidii
Cotoneaster horizontalis
Deutzia
Escallonia
Kerria
Lonicera pileata
Prunus laurocerasus
'Otto Luyken'
Viburnum tinus
Vinca

Growing a sunflower

Sunflowers *(Helianthus annuus)* are some of the easiest plants for children to grow. The seeds are large and easy for the smallest of fingers to hold. They grow quickly and you can choose between traditional tall or dwarf types.

1 Fill a container with a hole in the base with potting mixture. Make a hole in the surface with a finger and pop in a seed.

2 Water in well, place the pot in a sunny position and wait for the seed to germinate. Use the dwarf variety 'Pacino' for pots.

3 A proud young gardener with a fully grown sunflower. Once the petals have dropped and the seeds have ripened, hang up the head for the birds to feed on.

The themed garden

A themed garden can also be a time-saving garden. It means that you can more easily focus your choice of plants, pots, paint, furniture and other accessories to suit your theme and avoid making impulse buys that look wrong (and have to be replaced) or do not thrive (plants that need moving or time-consuming attention). But before you decide on a theme, it is important to assess the garden. For example, a hot and sunny aspect would lend itself to a Mediterranean theme, whereas a north-facing, shady garden could be made into a fern garden. A sheltered, semi-shaded spot is ideal for a Japanese-style garden.

A theme need not involve the whole garden. There may be a spot with problems that can be turned to your advantage. Instead of an entirely Mediterranean garden, transform a hot dry corner simply by selecting plants that enjoy the sun. Similarly, a shady corner could become the fern garden and a semi-shady paved area would suit a Japanese feature. And once you have chosen your theme, be sure to use appropriate plants – a lupin will look out of place in a Japanese garden and a rhododendron will be extremely unhappy in a hot, Mediterranean-style garden.

With a little imagination, you can reinvent your garden with a new colour or a planting theme. Consider creating a scented border near the patio or planting beds with a themed colour scheme. You will need to look at the garden with a critical eye to assess what is suitable. Do not seek to make major changes, but to adapt to any given situation.

A fern garden

If there is a shady corner in the garden, think about creating a fernery. You can transform a dark and miserable corner into a plot full of lush foliage with different shapes and textures. Most of the suitable plants enjoy a damp atmosphere; adding a small water feature will not only recreate a Victorian atmosphere, but will also provide extra humidity for the plants. A small statue adds a focal point; painting a modern concrete piece with yoghourt encourages a weathered look.

Plant suggestions:
Asplenium
Dryopteris
Fatsia japonica
Hedera
Helleborus
Matteuccia
Osmunda
Polypodium
Vinca minor
Viola

Right: The green foliage of the ferns and other shade-loving plants has been highlighted by the addition of a small statue. Figurines of goddesses add a Victorian touch to the fern garden.

The scented border

There is no better way to unwind after a busy day than to sit in a garden filled with sweet fragrance on a warm summer evening. Use a combination of shrubs, bedding plants and annuals. Annual seeds can be scattered directly into the soil. Even if there is very little space in the garden, one or two of the suggested plants flowering close to the patio will fill the air with scent.

Plant suggestions:

Heliotropium

Malcomia maritima (Virginia stock)

Matthiola bicornis (night-scented stock)

Mignonette

Nicotiana affinis

Daphne odora

Elaeagnus ebbingei

Jasminum officinale

Lonicera japonica 'Halliana'

Philadelphus

Above: *This border, planted with roses, philadelphus and honeysuckle, will provide scent and colour from late spring until early autumn. Also use plants with aromatic foliage, such as lavender and thyme.*

Right: *Old-fashioned, scented sweet peas* (Lathyrus odorata) *can be trained up a pyramid of canes or even allowed to ramble through shrubs. Pick them regularly to encourage further flowering.*

A Mediterranean garden

Ideally, you need well-drained soil for this type of planting to avoid waterlogging in the winter. The plants will need to be well-watered in their first year to enable them to establish, but after that they need very little attention. Mulching with gravel will not only give the garden a Mediterranean feel, but will also help to conserve moisture in the soil. For an extra sunny, southern look use plants such as agave in terracotta pots, which can be taken indoors for the winter. Most plants with silver foliage will also do well in this situation.

Plant suggestions:
Artemisia
Cistus
Convolvulus cneorum
Helianthemum
Lavandula
Nerine
Osteospermum
Phlomis
Phormium
Rosmarinus
Thymus

Below: A row of brightly coloured pelargoniums in terracotta pots will instantly bring the Mediterranean to your patio. The impatiens in the wall pots, which are in partial shade, echo the colour of the pelargoniums.

A *Japanese garden*

With strategically placed plants, a semi-shady spot that is perhaps looking rather bare can be transformed into a serene and simple oriental garden. Keep planting to a minimum and use gravel instead of grass. Use stone lanterns, chimes and bamboo to emphasise that oriental look.

Plant suggestions:

Acer palmatum
Camellia japonica
Hakonechloa macra 'Alboaurea'
Nandina
Ophiopogon planiscapus 'Nigrescens'
Pinus mugo 'Winter Gold'
Pleioblastus auricomus (syn. *Arundinaria auricoma*)
Pleioblastus humilis var. *pumilus*
    (syn. *Arundinaria pumila*)
Rhododendron himantodes 'Hinomayo'
Rhododendron 'Moerheim'

All these plants can be grown in pots and as some will require lime-free potting mixture, growing them in containers will allow you to provide them with the correct growing medium.

Above: *Bamboo edging, here used in front of an existing border, gravel and pebbles are all typical elements of a Japanese garden. Rake the gravel to give the impression of running water.*

Below: *Using an existing gravel path and adding some pebbles and a stone lantern, just one corner of this garden has been given an oriental look.*

Index

Credits

The majority of the photographs featured in this book have been taken by Geoffrey Rogers and are © Bookmart Publishing.

The publishers would like to thank the following photographers for providing images, credited here by page number and position: B(Bottom), T(Top), C(Centre), BL(Bottom Left), etc.

Eric Crichton: Copyright page, 23(R), 24(TR), 25(TC,TL), 28(L,R), 29(L,C,R), 31(BL), 35(T), 37(BR), 47(BR), 51(BR), 86(BL), 87(TL), 91(T)

John Glover: 6, 15(TR), 27(TR), 31(BR), 32(B), 33(T), 34(L,R), 59(CL), 88, 90

S & O Mathews: Half-title page, 14(C), 45(BL,BR), 51(CL), 52(BL), 53(T), 89(T,BR)

Clive Nichols Photos: 50(B), 52(T,Graham Strong), 53(BL,Sue Berger), 66(BL) Garden and security lighting), 67(T,Lisette Pleasance), 67(BL,Garden and security lighting), 91(B,Clive Nichols/J. Dowle & K. Ninomiya, Chelsea 9)

Geoffrey Rogers: 28(C), 25(TR,B)

Neil Sutherland © Geoffrey Rogers: 23(L,C), 24(TC,BL,BC)

Acknowledgements

The publishers would like to thank the following people and organisations for their help during the preparation of this book: Zoë Belcher and family; Decco Glosters, Woking; Fragbarrow Nurseries, Ditchling, East Sussex; J & J Plants, Dorset; Dennis and Hilda Freedman; Jan Kraatz (Interplants) Holland; Murrells Nursery, West Sussex; The Old Basket Company, London; Graham Quick; William Rogers; Shore Hall Garden Designs; Chris Newnham at Washington Garden Centre, West Sussex; Woodlodge Products, Walton-on-Thames.